SUPER BIG! SUPER VALUE!
SUPER FUN!
Coloring & Activity Book

©2006 Learning Horizons, One American Road, Cleveland, OH 44144 Made in USA

Mini Storybooks:

Throughout the book, you'll find mini storybooks that are designed to be removed and read aloud. Ask your child to first color the story pages inside the book. Then, help your child make each of these little storybooks by following these simple directions:

1. Remove the two pages.

2. Cut along the dotted lines.

3. Fold the pages in half, one tucked inside the other.

4. Staple pages together at center.

Flash cards:

This book contains one complete set of flash cards for numbers 1 to 20. The front of each flash card presents the numeral and a corresponding number of pictures. The back of each flash card presents the numeral, the number word (to *ten*) and a corresponding number of circles for your child to color in. Help your child make this useful set of flash cards by following these simple directions.

1) With the pages still inside the book, ask your child to color the pictures on the front of each flash card and the circles on the back of each flash card.

2) Tear out the pages along the perforated edges.

3) Help your child to cut along the dotted lines to create four double-sided cards out of each page.

What begins with **c**?

Camels are **c**ool!

Color. Circle each **C** or **c**.

Cats like **c**ars!

Color Key

C = blue   **c** = orange

A = yellow   **a** = red

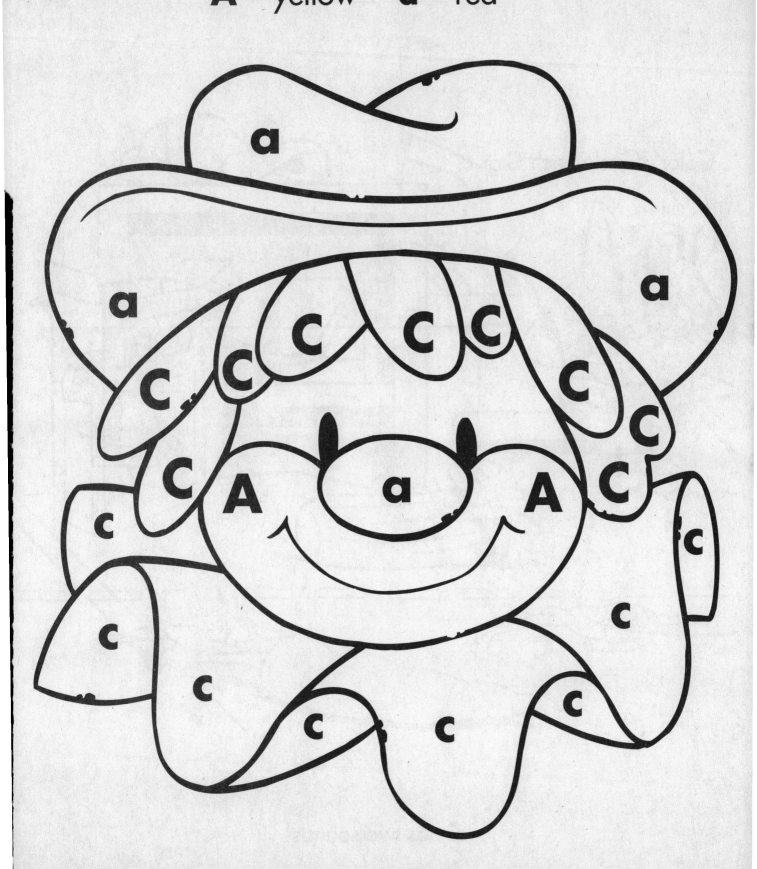

Color. Circle what begins with **c** as in .

C has two sounds!

Color. Draw lines to match by the **c** sound.

Can you hear two sounds of **c**?

Follow the **ABC** path.

Dd

Dinosaur **D**an

Follow what begins with **d** to help the 🐕 get to the 🏠.

Dragon sits at a **d**esk.

Color. Circle each **D** or **d**.

Dogs **d**o **d**aring feats!

Ee

What begins with **e**?

Elephants are **e**normous!

Enchanting **e**ggs!

Color. Circle each **E** or **e**.

Exciting **e**lephants!

What begins with **f**?

Fanny Frog

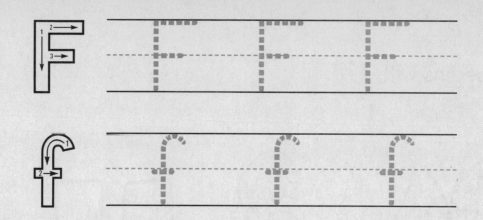

Color. Circle each **F** or **f**.

Find the **f**ish!

Color. Find and circle 5 **F**'s.

Flamingos are **f**un!

Follow the **a b c d e f** path.

Connect the dots from **a** to **f**.

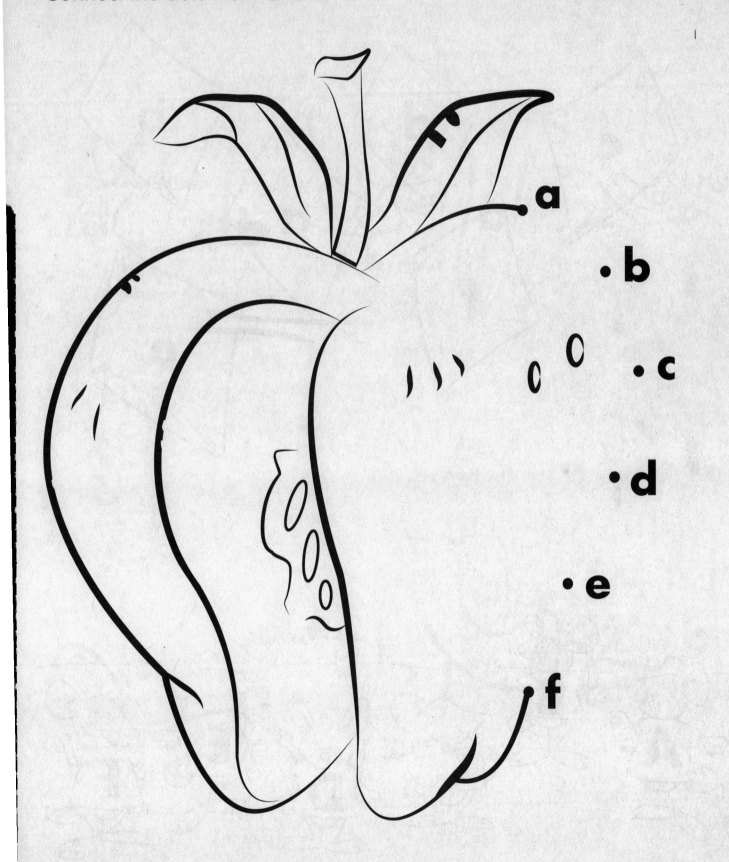

Draw a string for each kite by matching letters.

What begins with **g** ?

Gg

Goat is at the **g**arden **g**ate.

Color Key

G or **g** = brown   **b** = red   **C** = yellow   **d** = orange

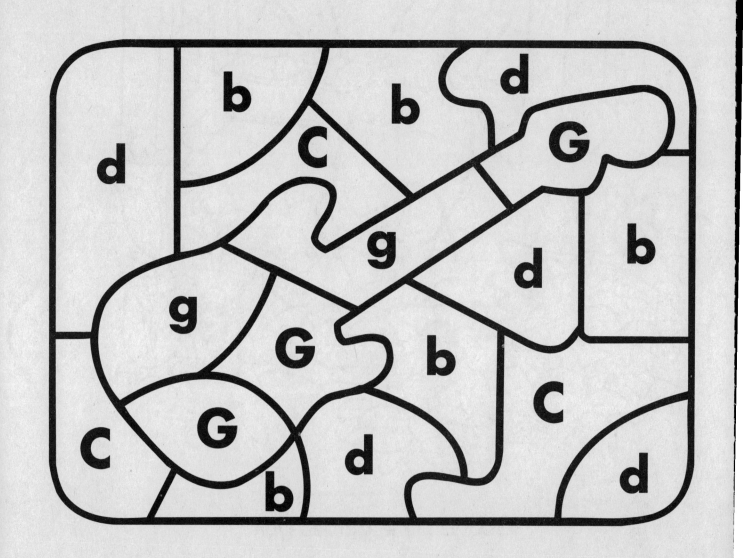

Color Key

G = blue   **g** = brown   **C** = red   **D** = yellow

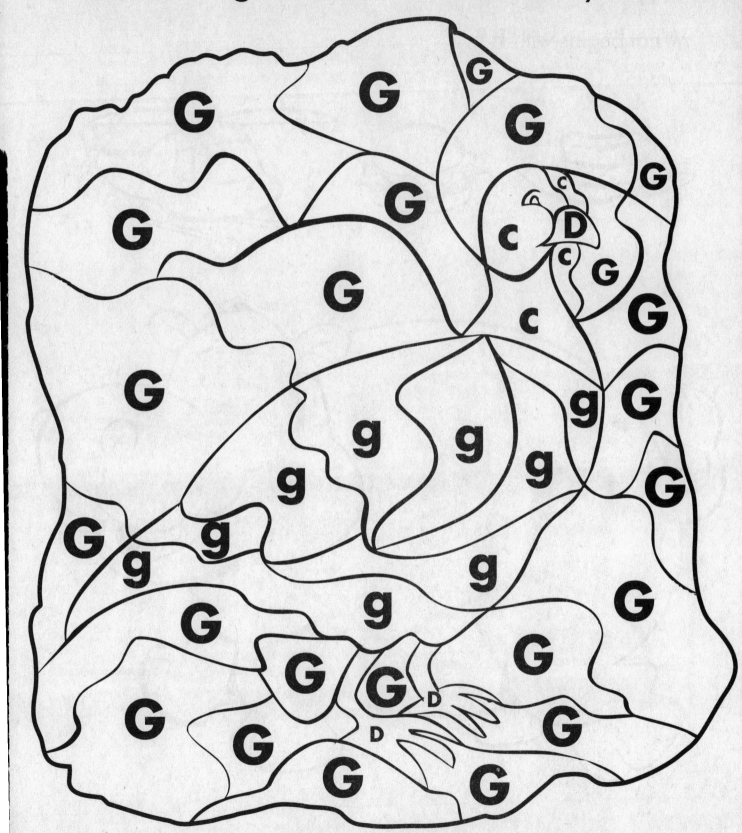

Gobble, gobble!

Hh

What begins with **h**?

Huge **h**ippo!

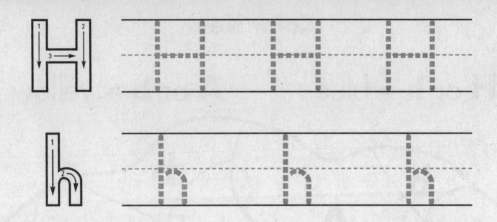

Follow the **Hh** path.

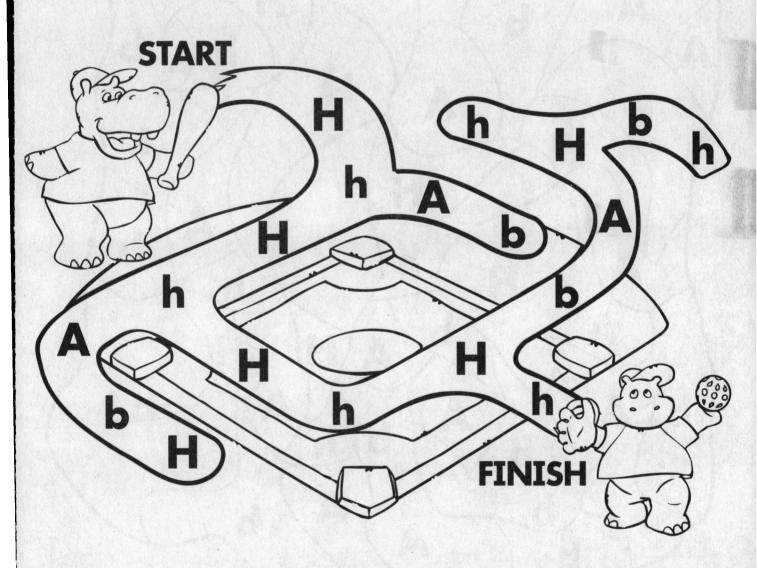

START

H

h

H

h

A

H

A

b

b

A

b

H

H

FINISH

h

h

b

Happy **h**ippos play ball!

Color Key

H or **h** = blue   **A** or **b** = yellow

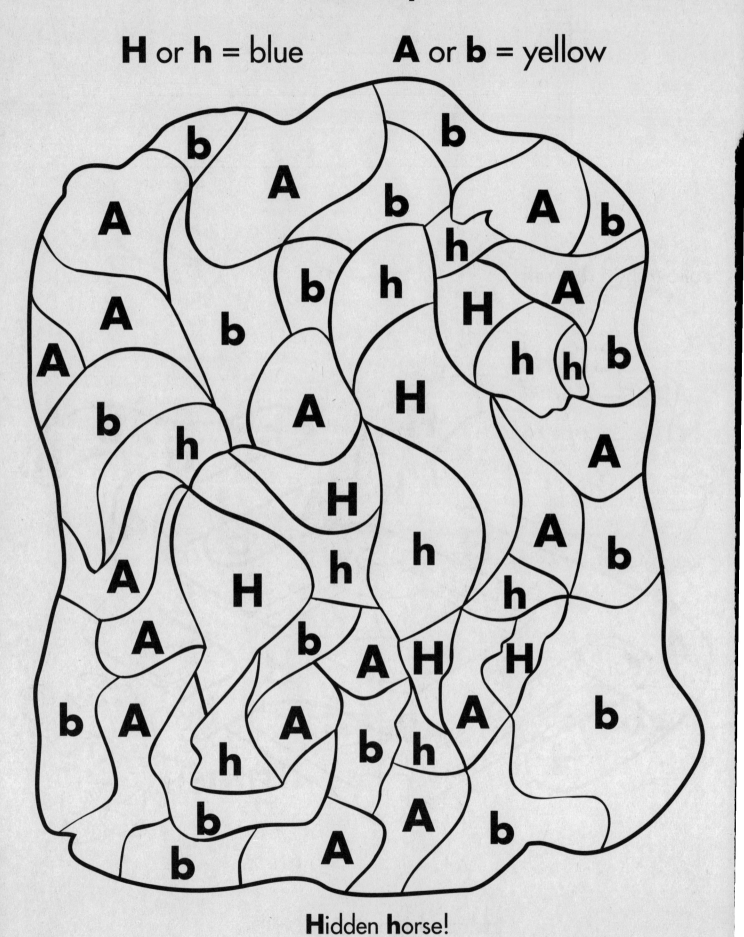

Hidden horse!

What begins with i?

Ii

Inchworm **is I**guana's friend!

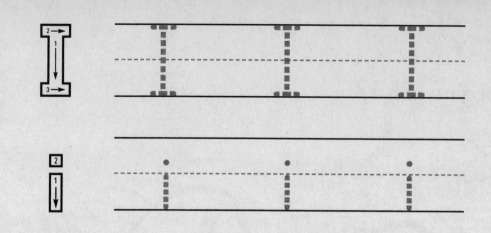

Color. Circle each **I** or **i**.

Ice cream **is** yummy!

Follow the **Ii** path.

Connect the dots from **A** to **I**.

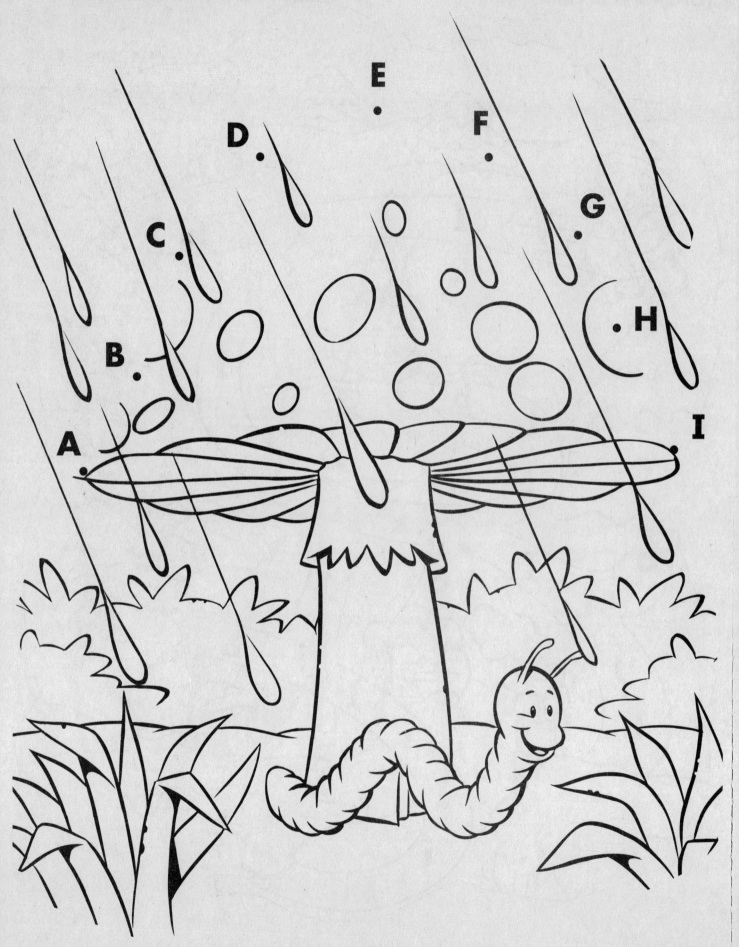

Jj

Jack-o-lanterns are **j**ust great!

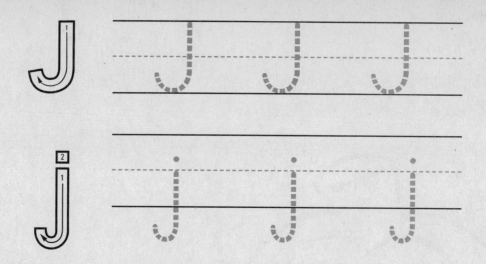

J

j

Color. Circle each **J** or **j**.

Jars of **j**elly

The **j**uggler **j**uggles **j**am, **j**acks, a **j**ug, a **j**et, and a **j**eep!

Kk

Kids love **k**ites!

K K K K

k k k k

Follow the **Kk** path.

START

FINISH

K k K k A h
h h A K k K
h k H k K k
A K K k K
h h K K h
K H K A
A h H A k
h A K k
K k

The **k**ing wants the **k**ey.

Color Key

K or **k** = blue   **A** or **h** = yellow

Find **Kk** in the kitchen.

Follow the path from **A** to **K**.

Connect the dots from **A** to **K**, then connect the dots from **a** to **k**.

What begins with **l**?

Ll

Lamb **l**eans against a **l**og.

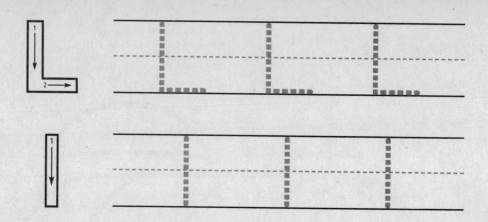

Color what begins with **l** yellow.

Lamb is on a **l**adder.   **L**ion drinks **l**emonade.

Color. Circle each **L** or **l**.

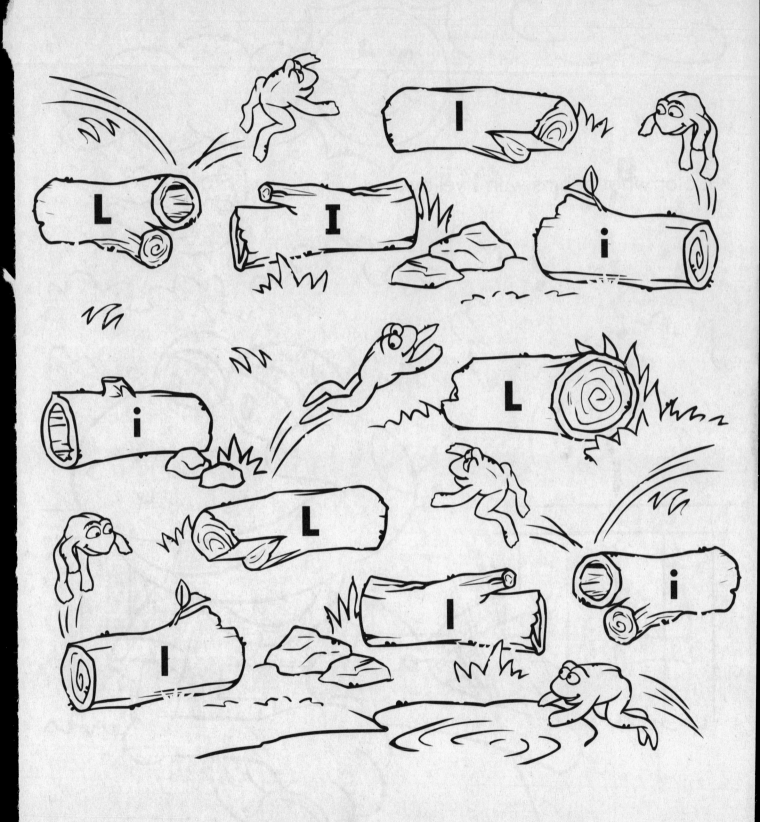

Frogs leap over logs.

Connect the dots from **a** to **l**.

Finish writing **A** to **L**.

Mm

Mouse is on a **m**otorcycle.

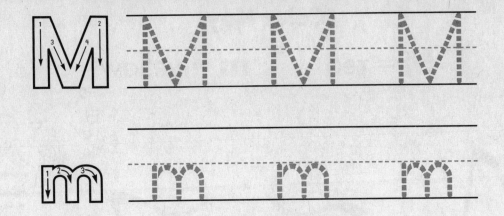

Follow the **Mm** path.

START

FINISH

Monkey needs his **m**ittens.

Color Key

M = red   **m** = yellow

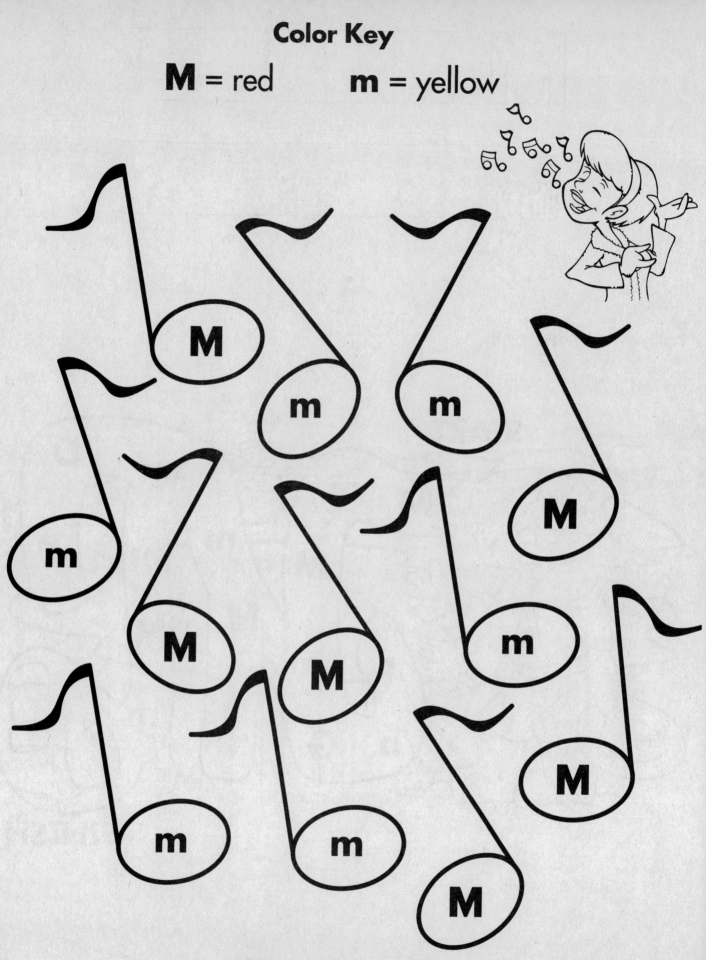

Mary **m**akes **m**usic.

Connect the dots from **a** to **m**.

Nn

Nest of **n**ine baby birds

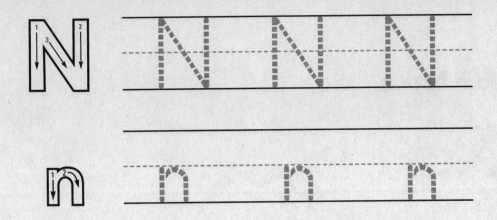

Color. Circle what begins with **n**.

Nurse **N**ancy

Circle each **N** or **n**.

Find **N** and **n** in the **n**oodles.

Color. Match **M** to **m** and **N** to **n**.

Nice Monsters!

Connect the dots from **e** to **n**.

Otters love the ocean!

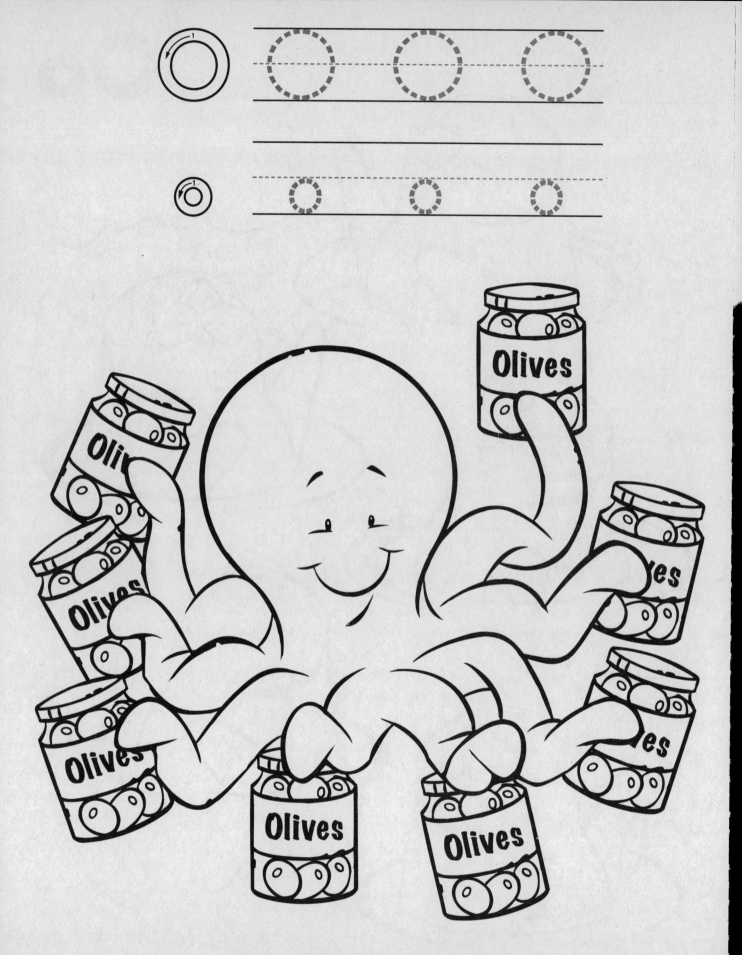

Oscar Octopus loves olives!

Color Key

O or **o** = purple   **a** or **c** = blue

Connect the dots from **A** to **O**.

Pp

Pig is in a **p**en.

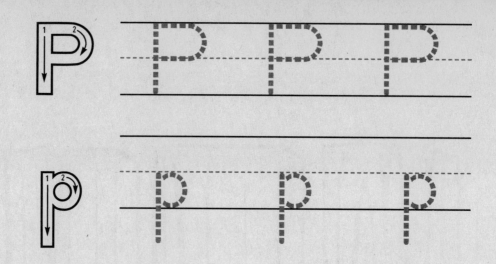

Color. Circle each **P** or **p**.

Penguins **p**lay in the snow.

What begins with **p**?

Pig **p**lays a **p**iano!

Connect the dots from a to p.

Queen **Q**uinn sits **q**uietly.

Qq

Color. Circle each **Q** or **q**.

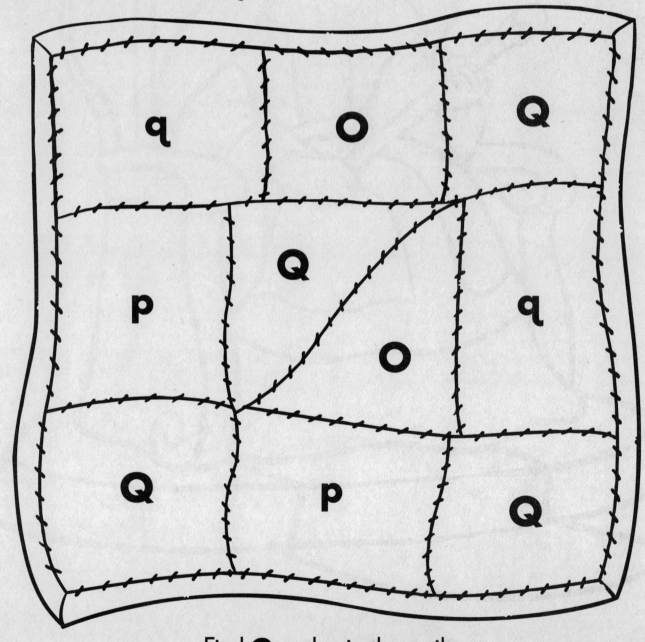

Find **Q** and **q** in the **q**uilt.

Connect the dots from **a** to **q**.

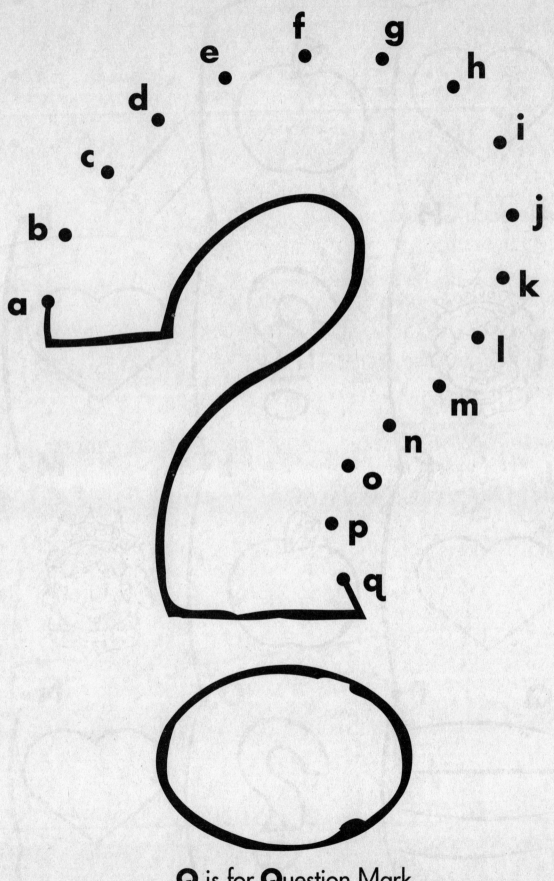

Q is for **Q**uestion Mark

Connect the dots from **A** to **Q**.

Connect the dots from **i** to **q**.

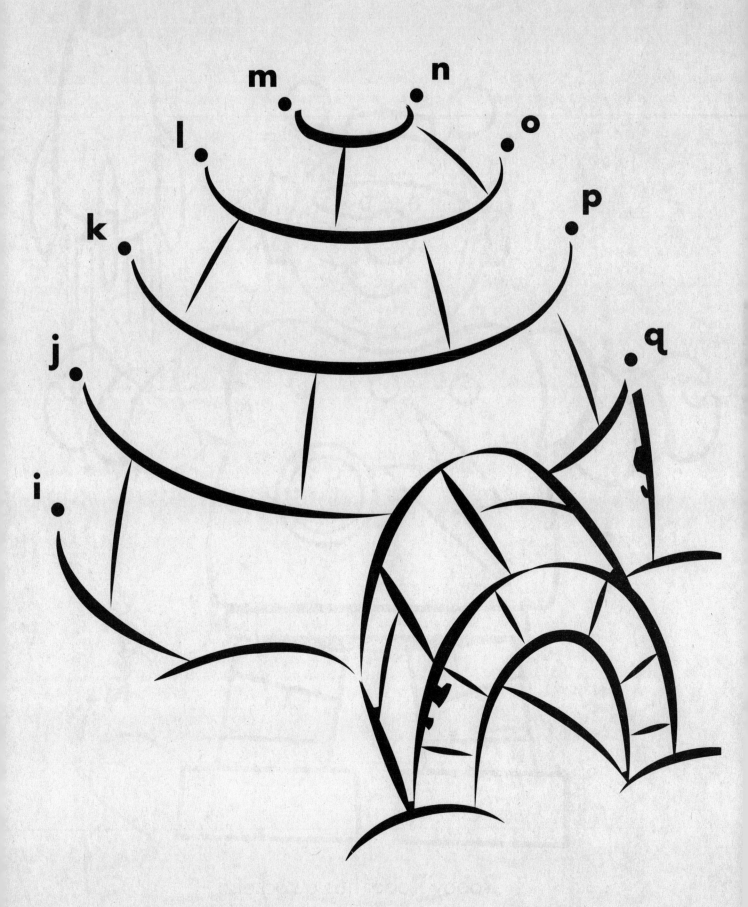

Rr

Robby **R**obot has a **r**ocket!

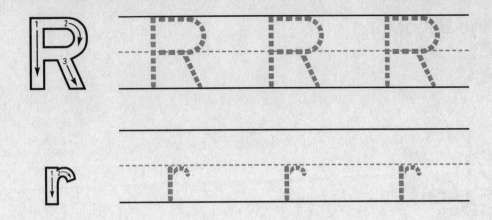

R R R R R

r r r r r

Color. Circle what begins with **r**.

Follow the **Rr** path.

Rabbit wants **r**adishes.

Ss

Seal **s**its in the **s**un.

S   S   S   S   S   S

s   s   s   s   s   s

Sam and **S**id **s**it on a **s**ee**s**aw.

Color. Circle each **S** or **s**.

Color. Circle 3  s.

Snakes **s**wim in the **s**ea.

Connect the dots from **a** to **s**.

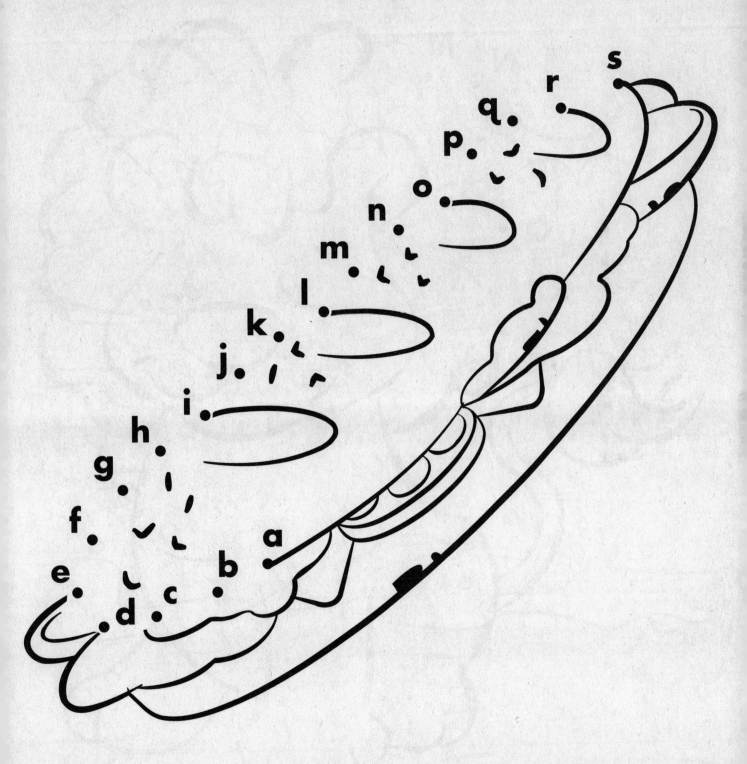

Connect the dots from **L** to **S**.

T t

What begins with **t**?

Tiger and **T**urtle have **t**oys and a **t**ent.

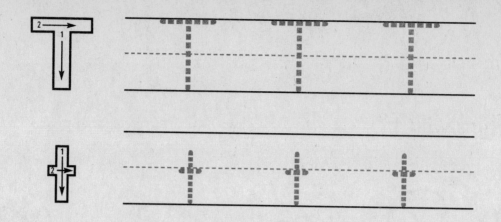

Color. Circle each **T** or **t**.

Connect the dots from **a** to **t**.

Turkey and **T**urtle see capital **T**!

Uu

Under **u**mbrellas

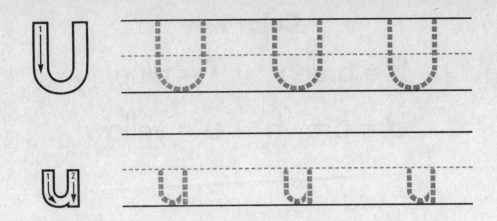

Color. Circle each **U** or **u**.

Color Key

S = green   **T** = blue

U = brown   **u** = yellow

Connect the dots from **k** to **u**.

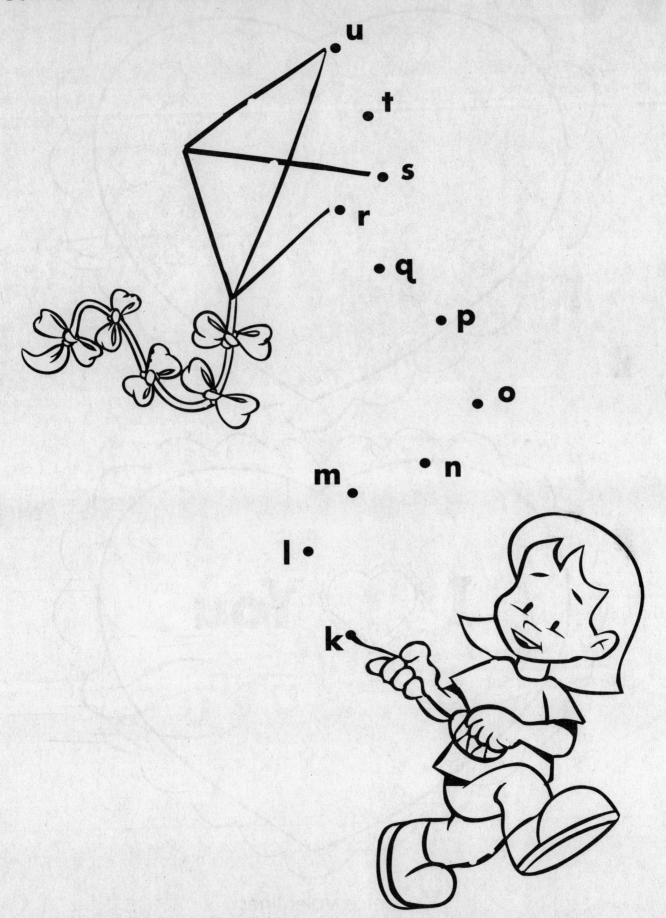

Vv

I ♥ You

Very nice **v**alentines!

V V V V V V V

V V V V V V V

Find:

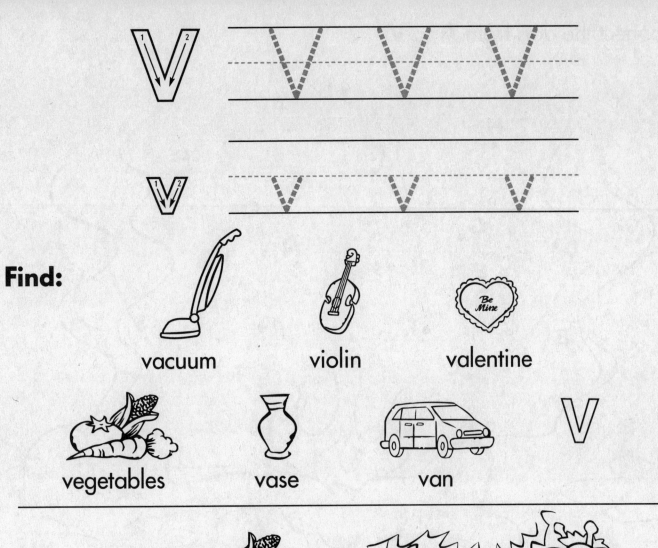

vacuum   violin   valentine

vegetables   vase   van

V

Connect the dots from **A** to **V**.

Vv is for **V**olcano.

Ww

Wendy **W**itch has a **w**and.

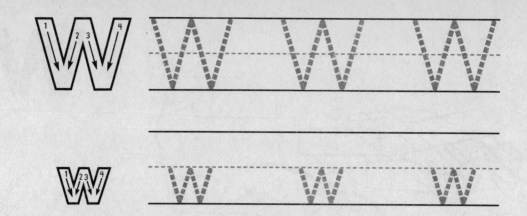

Color. Circle what begins with **w**.

Color. Circle each **W** or **w**.

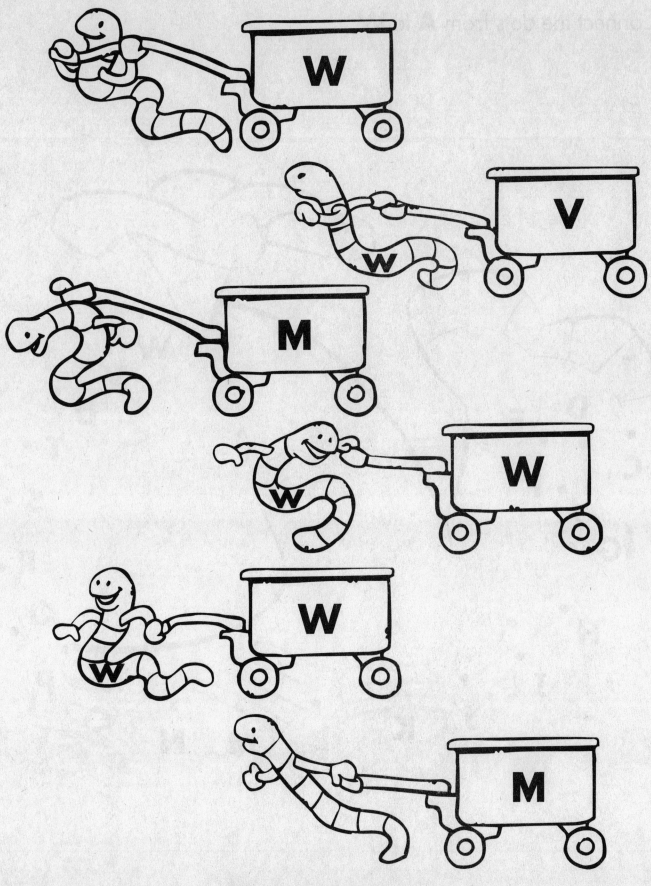

Worms pull **w**agons.

Connect the dots from **A** to **W**.

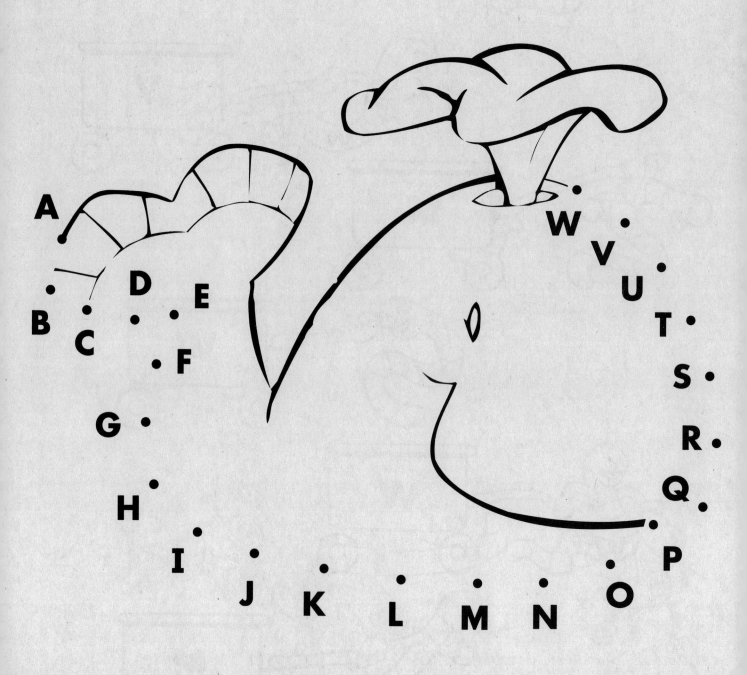

Follow the path from **a** to **w**.

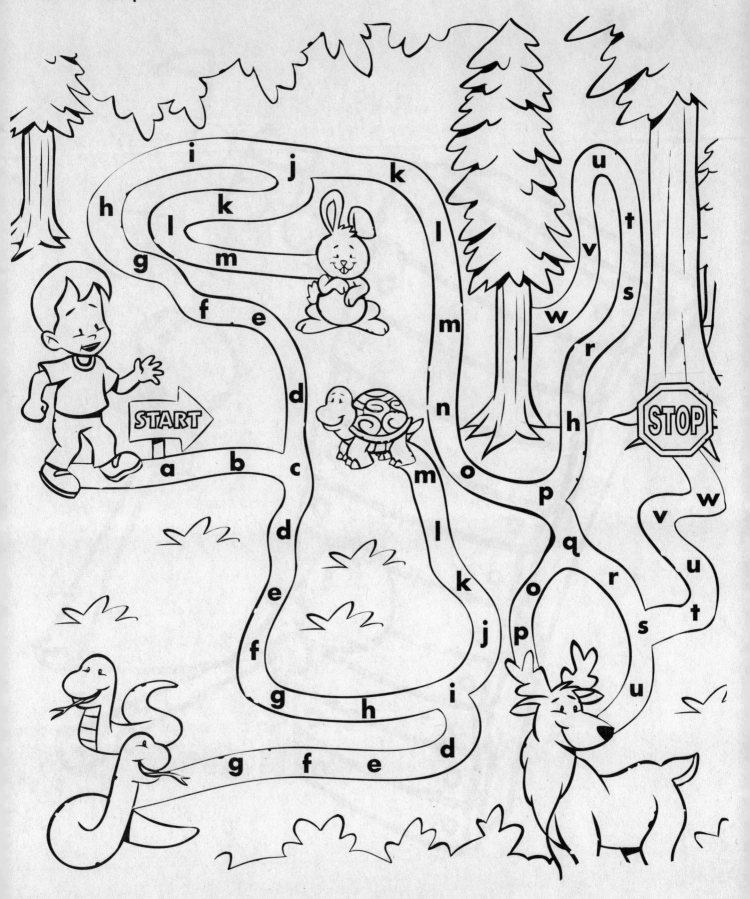

Andy **w**alks through the **w**oods.

Xx

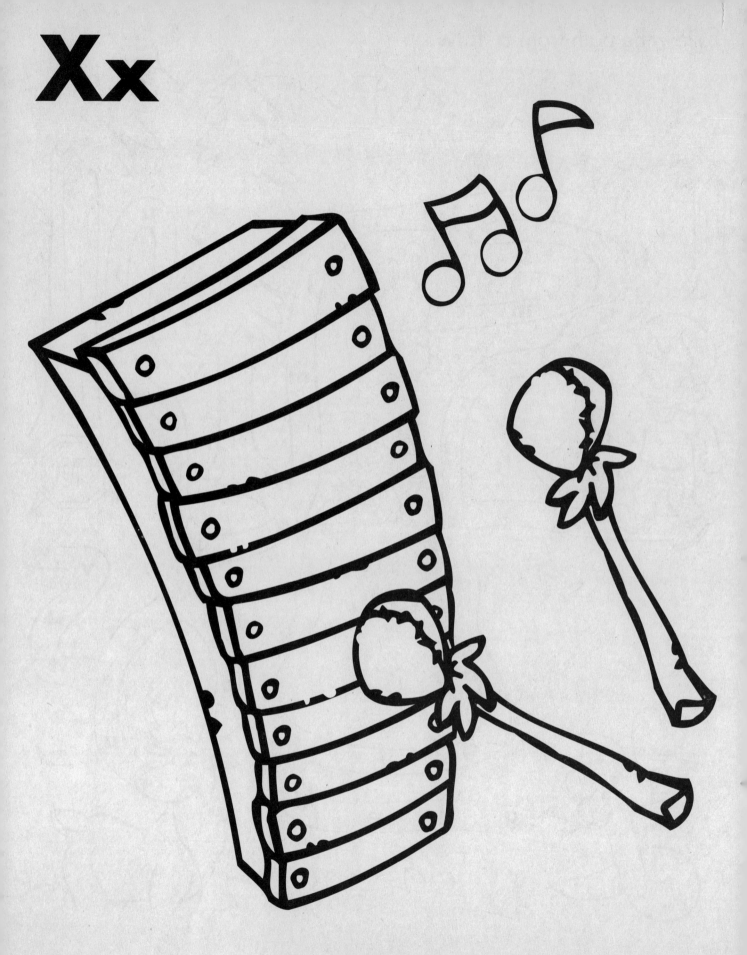

Xx is for **X**ylophone.

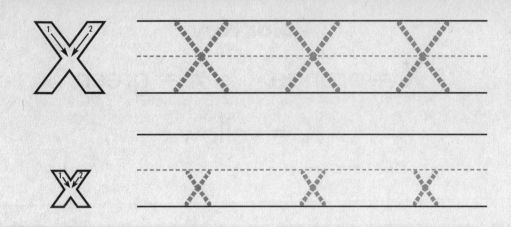

Match the **x**-rays.

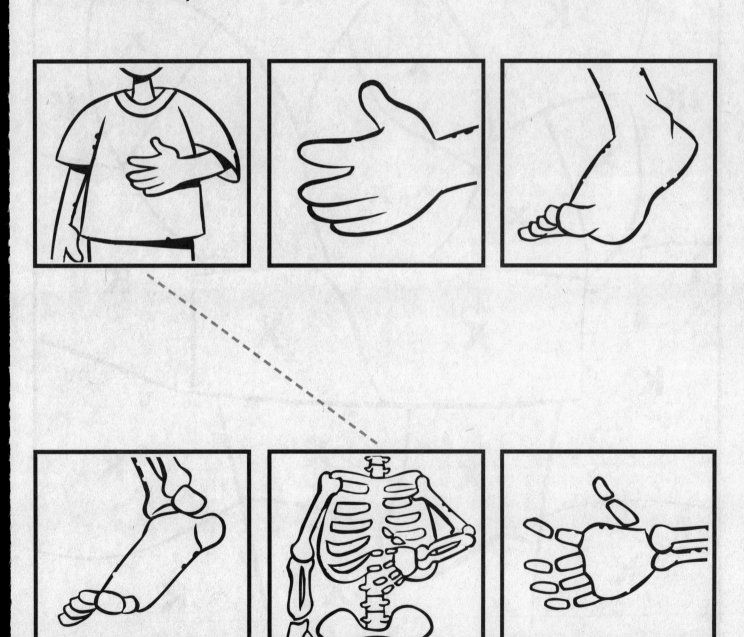

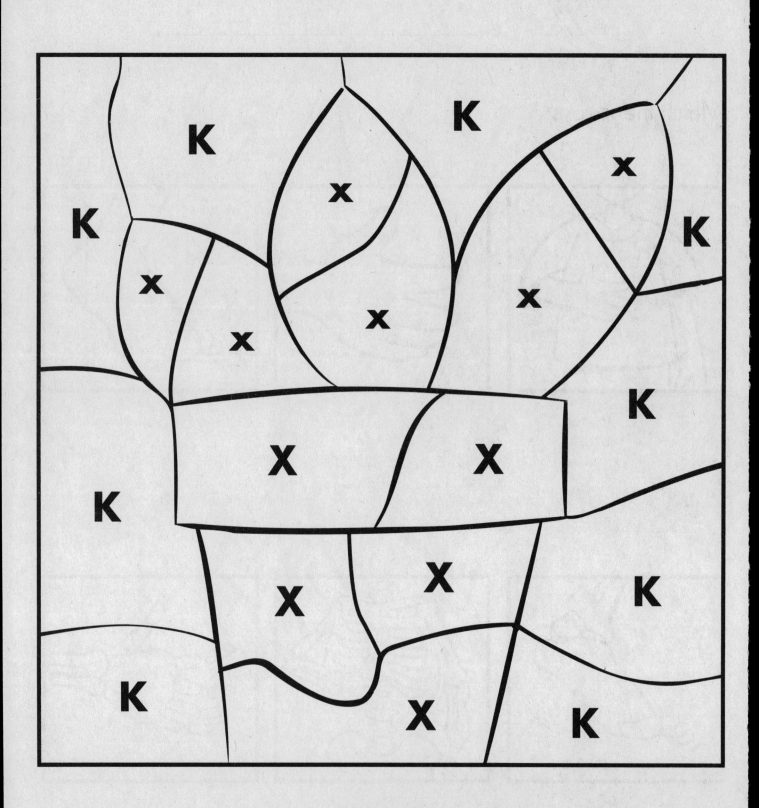

Yy

Yolanda Yak

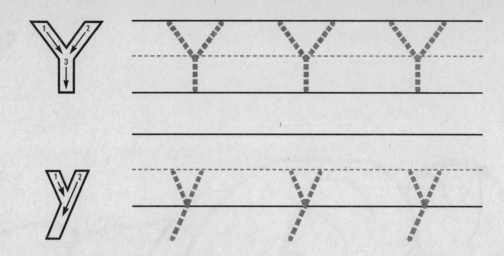

Color what begins with **y** yellow. Color the rest red.

Yy is for **y**ellow, **y**olk, **y**awn, **y**o-**y**o, and **y**arn.

Color. Circle each **Y** or **y**.

Yak has a **yo-y**o.

Zz

Zz is for **Z**oo.

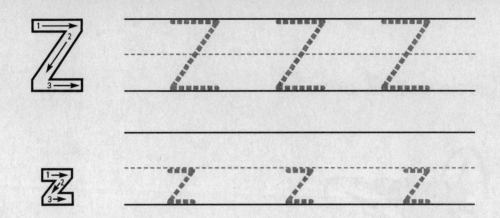

Color. Circle what begins with **z**.

Zz is for **z**ero, **z**ipper, and **z**ebra.

Color. Circle each **Z** or **z**.

Find 5  s.

LION

Connect the dots from **A** to **Z**.

Connect the dots from **h** to **z**.

Find and circle **F O X**.

Find and circle **F L O A T**.

Find and circle **B C D H L M R T V Y**.

Follow the path from **A** to **Z**.

Follow the path from **a** to **z**.

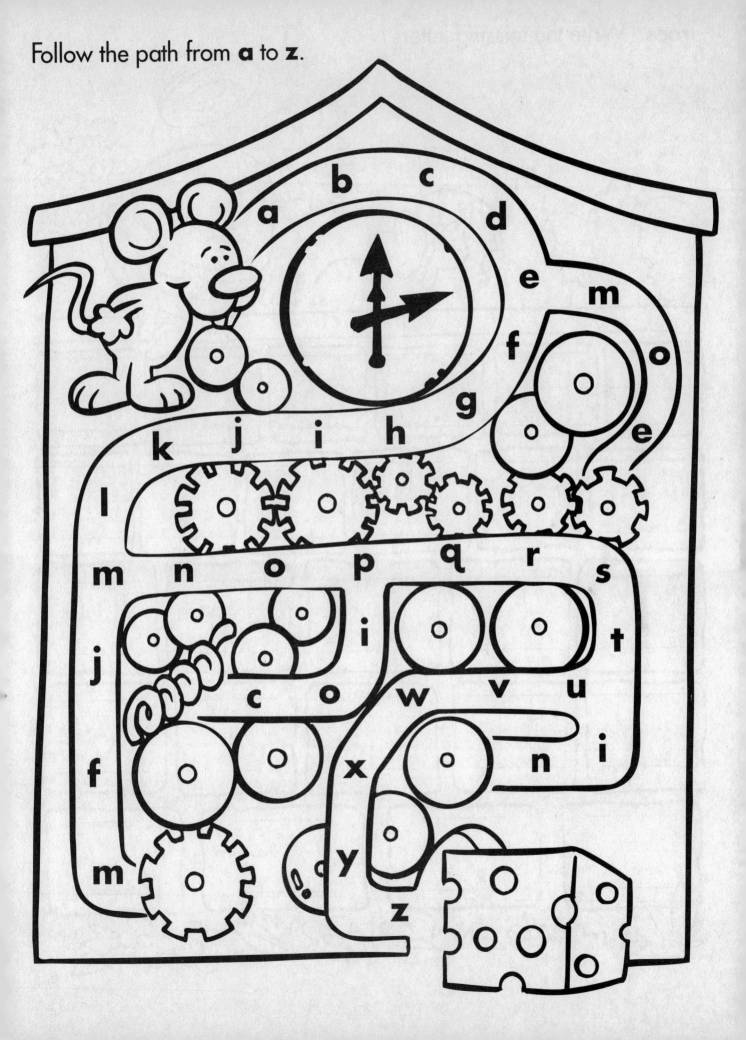

Trace. Write the missing letters.

Connect the dots from **a** to **z**.

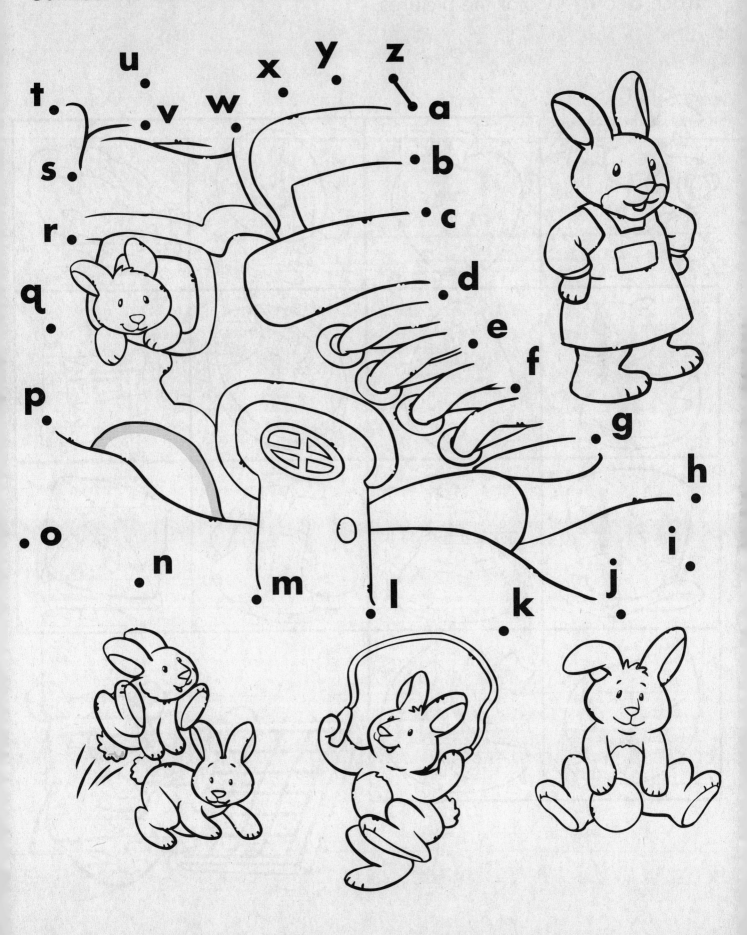

Trace **a** to **m**. Color the pictures.

Trace **n** to **z**. Color the pictures.

You are an alphabet champ!
Write your name. Color the ribbon blue.

Congratulations _____ **!**

Aa   Kk   Mm   Ss

    Zz   Bb
Ii

                    GREAT

Cc   JOB!   Jj

                                            Tt
Ll
    Uu   Qq
                                          Ee
Oo   Dd
                                        Yy

    Xx   Gg

Ff

                                                    Vv
    Nn
              Hh   Pp   Rr
Ww

Color Key

a = orange   **e** = blue   **i** = red

o = purple   **u** = green   ★ = yellow

Cat has a hat.
Cat has a bag.

The **a**nts h**a**ve **a**n **a**pple!

Color, then write **a** to finish each word.

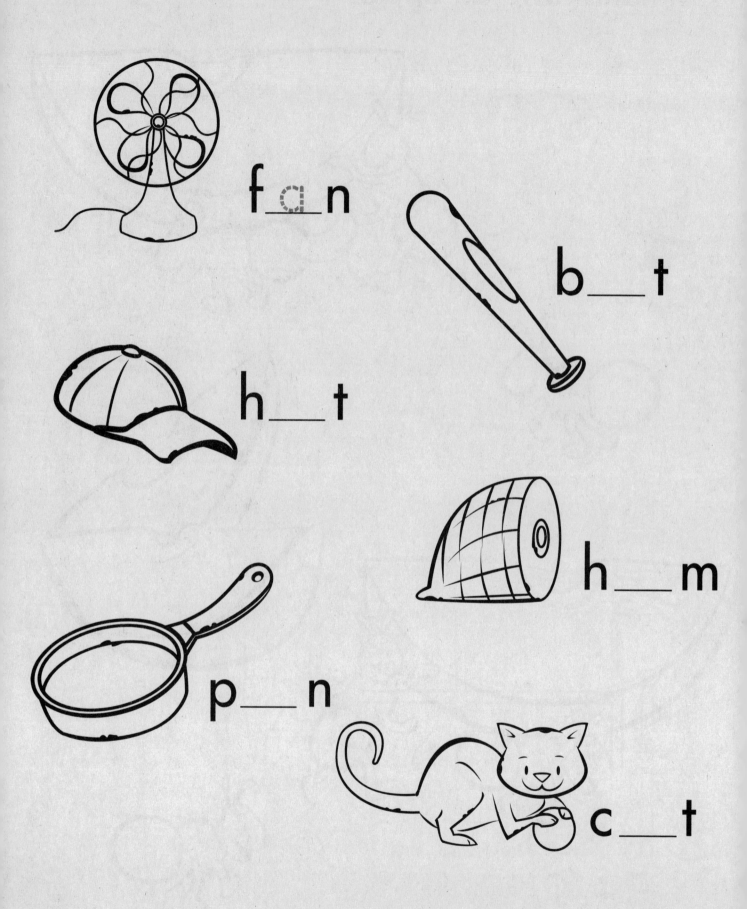

f_a_n

b__t

h__t

h__m

p__n

c__t

CAT MAN

But one thing Cat Man does
not have - RATS!

This is Cat Man and his
cats, cats, cats.

Cat Man has cats with fans
and cats with hats.

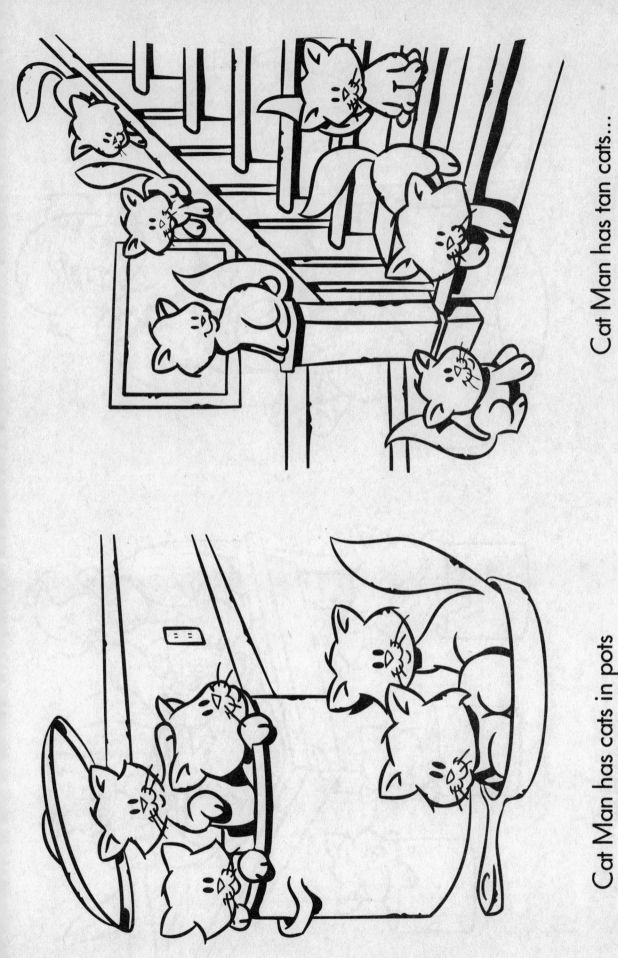

Cat Man has cats in pots and pans.

Cat Man has tan cats....

and fat cats.

Cats on mats.
Cats in cans.

Ella **El**ephant is in b**e**d.

Ed has **te**n **pe**ts.

Color, then write **e** to finish each word.

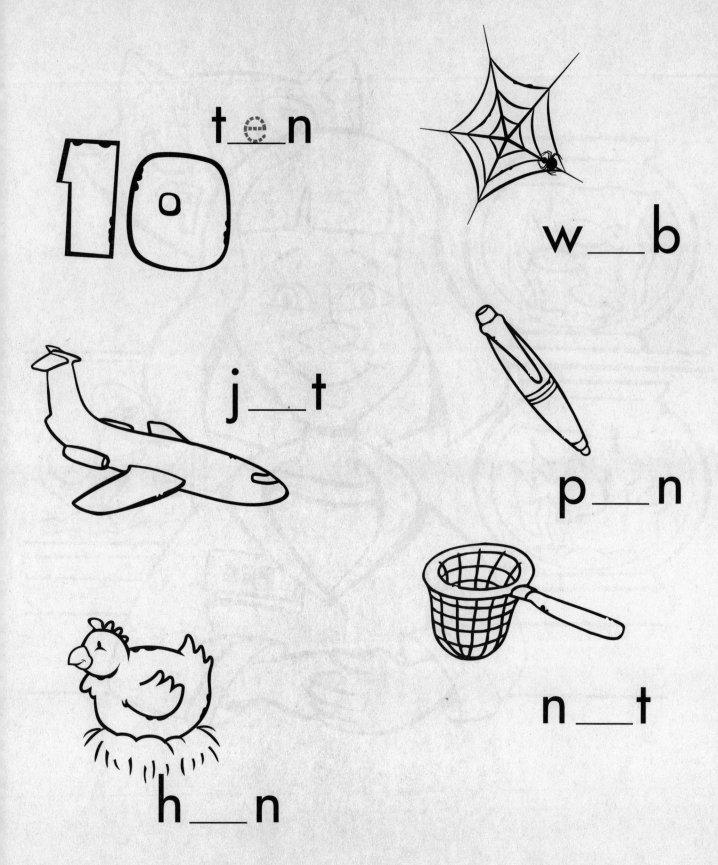

t__n

10

o

w__b

j__t

p__n

n__t

h__n

Peg sells pets.

My Wet Hen

This is Ben...

This is Ben,
his wet hen,
and a wet Ken!

and his pet hen.

and his wet hen.

This is Ken.

This is Ben....

Look out, Ben!

Look out for Ken!

Izzy is a pig.
This pig is big.

The **infant** **is** under a quilt.

Iguana is in the kitchen.

Color, then write **i** to finish each word.

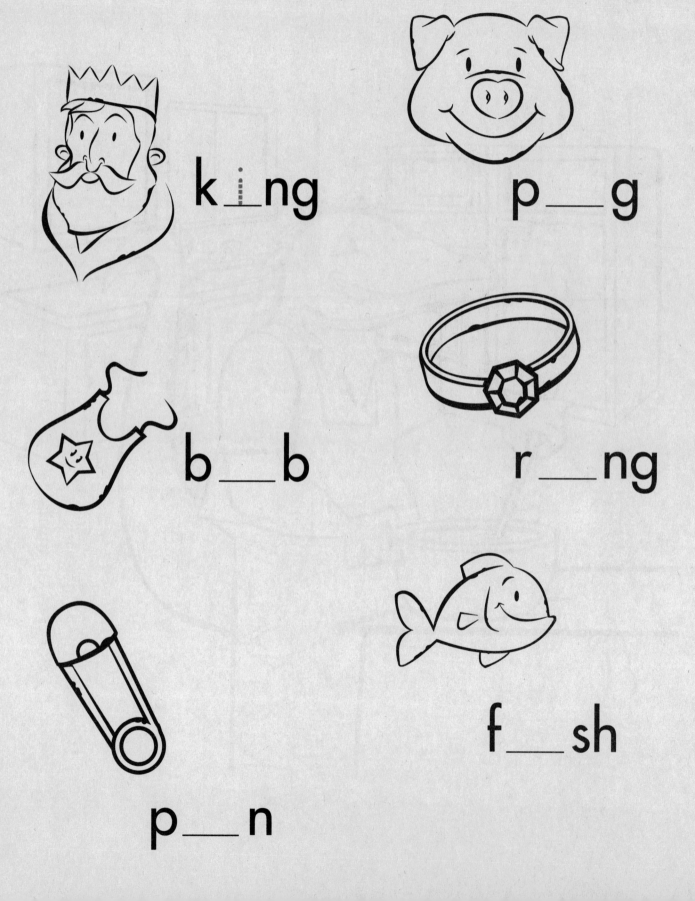

k i ng

p __ g

b __ b

r __ __ ng

p __ __ n

f __ sh

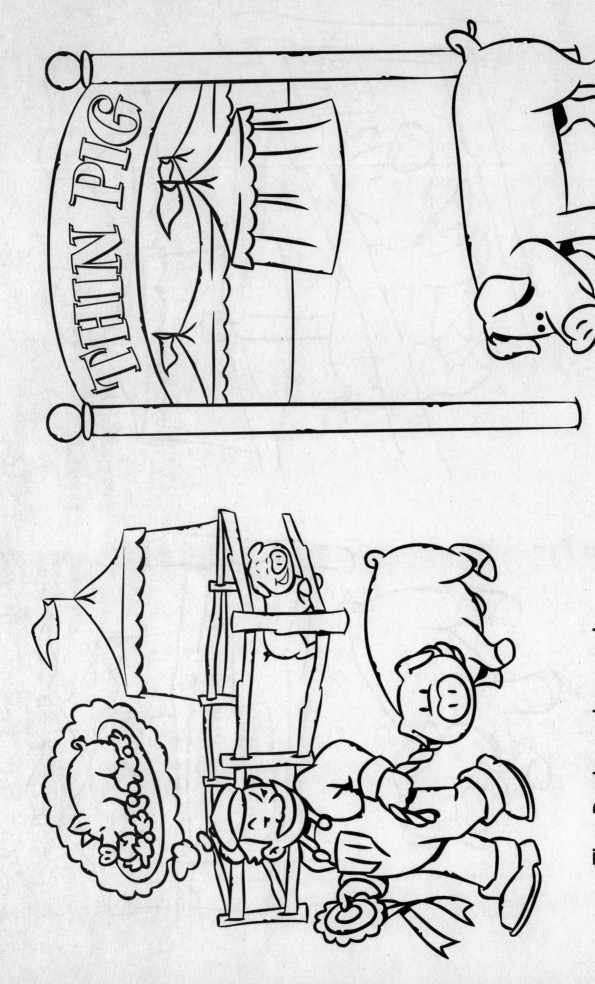

Thin Pig has a big grin!
It can be good to be thin!

8

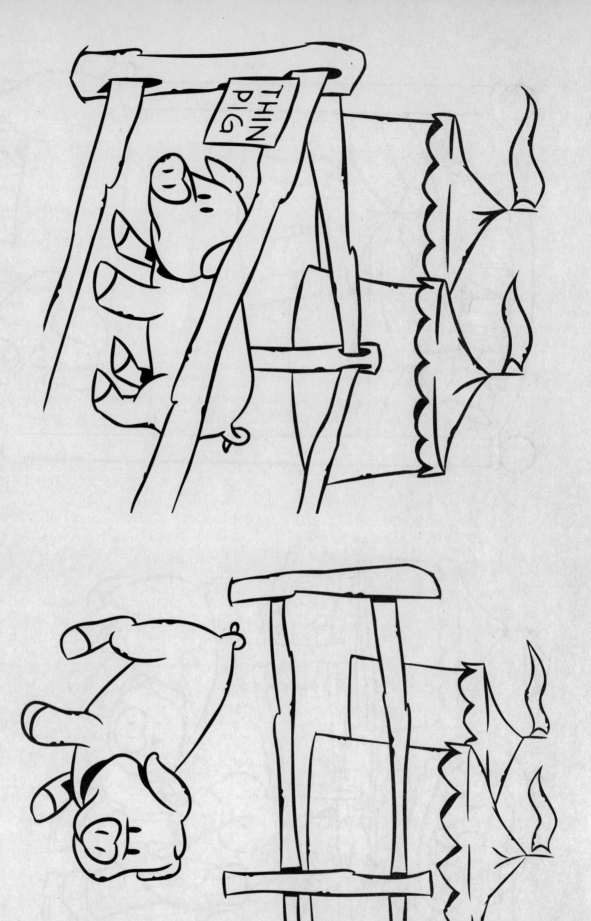

Thin Pig

Thin Pig did not win.

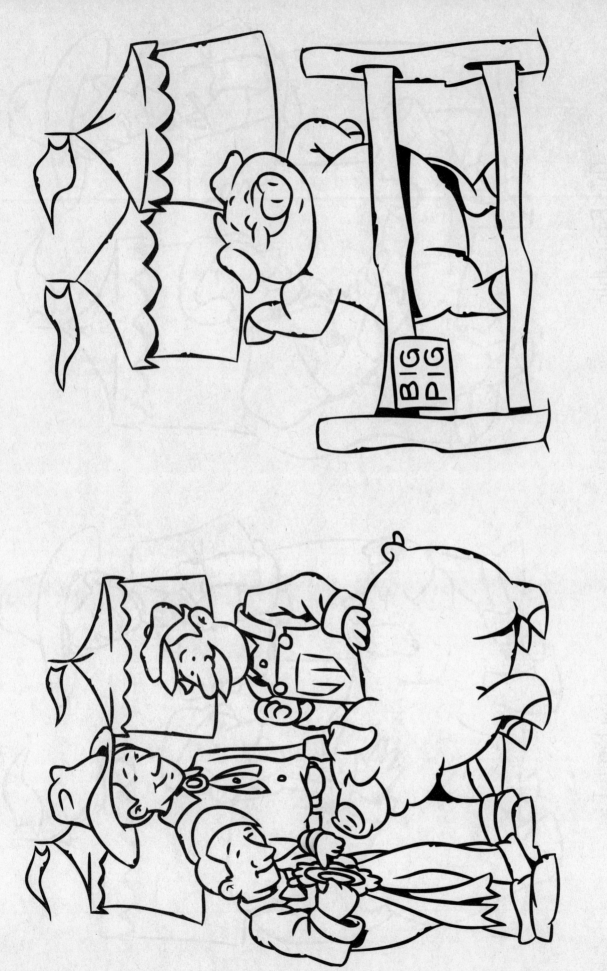

Big Pig

Big Pig wins.

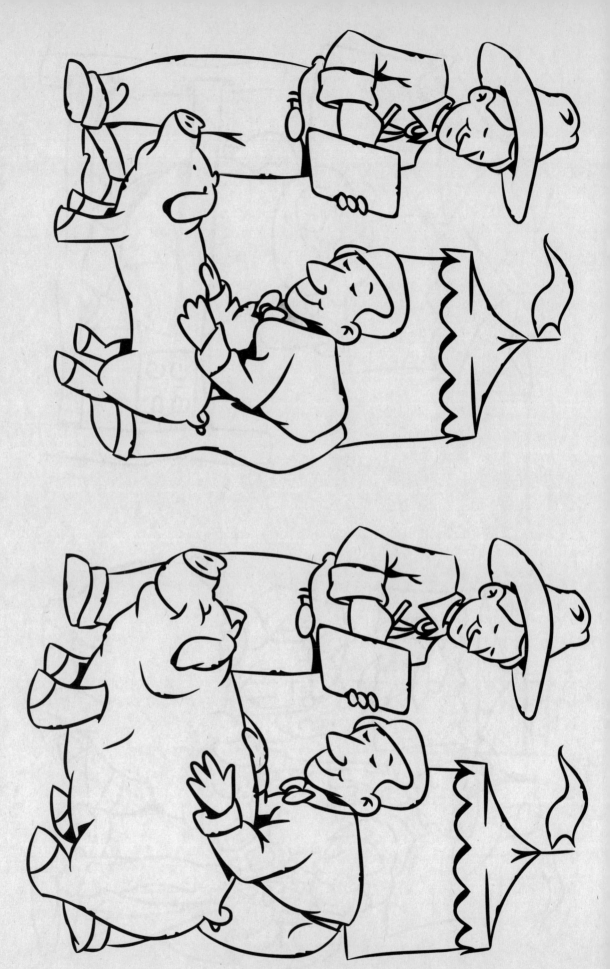

Thin Pig is thin,
thin, thin.

Big Pig is big,
big, big.

4 5

Dot and Bob hop and hop.

A frog is **on** a log.

Oscar the dog says, "Stop!"

Color, then write o to finish each word.

cl o ck

d __ ll

p __ t

bl __ ck

t __ p

s __ ck

Top Hog

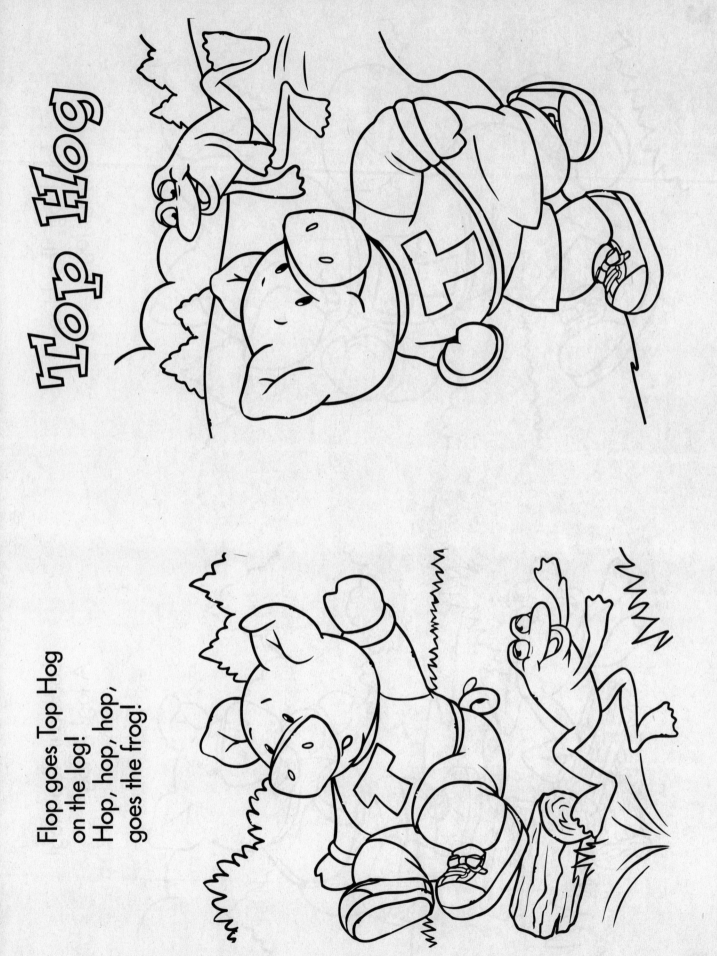

Flop goes Top Hog
on the log!
Hop, hop, hop,
goes the frog!

Top Hog, Top Hog,
jog, jog, jog!

Look out, Top Hog!
A log! A log!

Chop, chop, Top Hog.
Chop that log!

Frog goes free!
Hop, hop, hop!

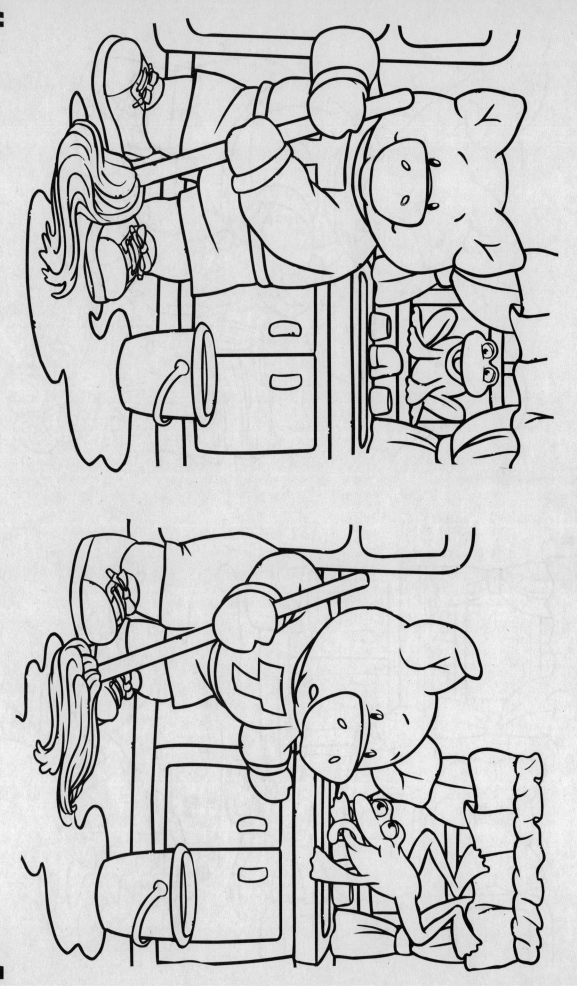

Top Hog, Top Hog,
mop, mop, mop!

Look out, Top Hog!
A frog! A frog!

Duck is in a tub.

Bug on a r**u**g
with a n**u**t and a c**u**p.

Ducks **u**nder **u**mbrellas!

Color, then write **u** to finish each word.

tr__ck

t__b

s__n

b__s

dr__m

c__p

HUG A CUB

Hug! Hug!
Give a bug a hug
at the Cub Club.

8

Hug a cub.
Hug a cub.

A bug! A bug!
A bug is in the Cub Club!

Hug a cub.
Hug a cub
at the Cub Club.

Hug a cub
at the Cub Club.

3

CUB CLUB

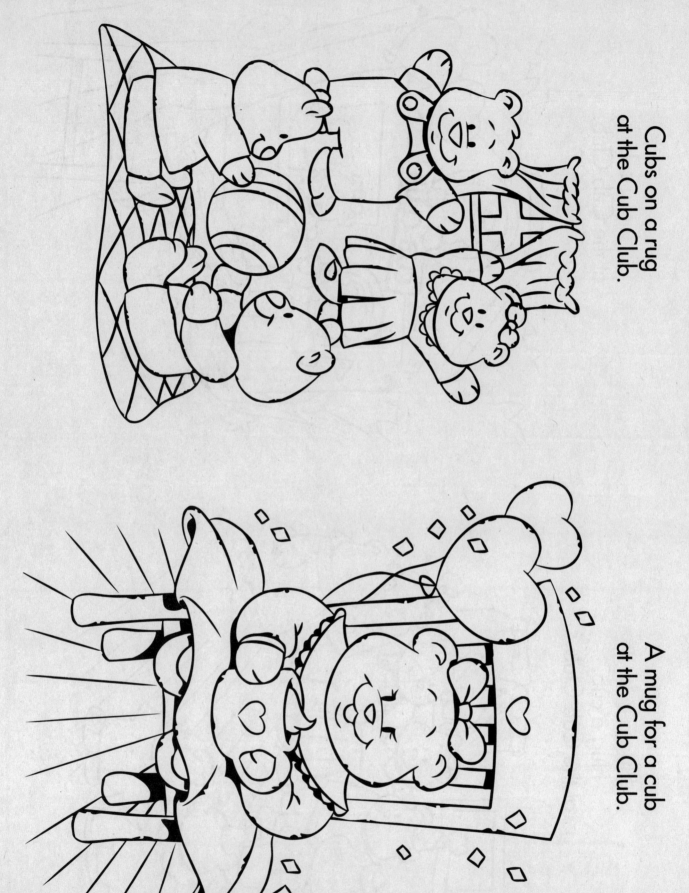

Cubs on a rug
at the Cub Club.

A mug for a cub
at the Cub Club.

Color Key

words with **a** = blue   words with **e** = brown

words with **i** = yellow   words with **o** = green

words with **u** = pink

it

tin

tub

sun

bus

wig

lip

is

jig

tip

sip

win

hop

on

bib

pin

big

hog

top

jog

in

pig

pet

net

pen

ten

bed

cat

ant

pan

hat

web

fan

cap

Find and circle each word.

H G F A N T

X P I G W Q

L O G M V R

W E B R U G

 **FAN**

 **WEB**

 **LOG**

 **PIG**

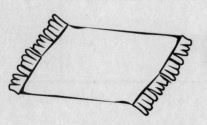 **RUG**

You are a short vowel sounds champ!
Write your name.
Color the trophy yellow.

_____

- -

Congratulations _____ !

i

o

a

u

SUPER!

e

Color everything **red**.

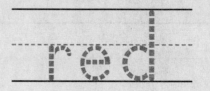

Color everything **yellow**.

yellow

A **red** and **yellow** friend!

Color everything **blue**.

blue

Color everything **green**.

green

Green and **blue** feathered friends!

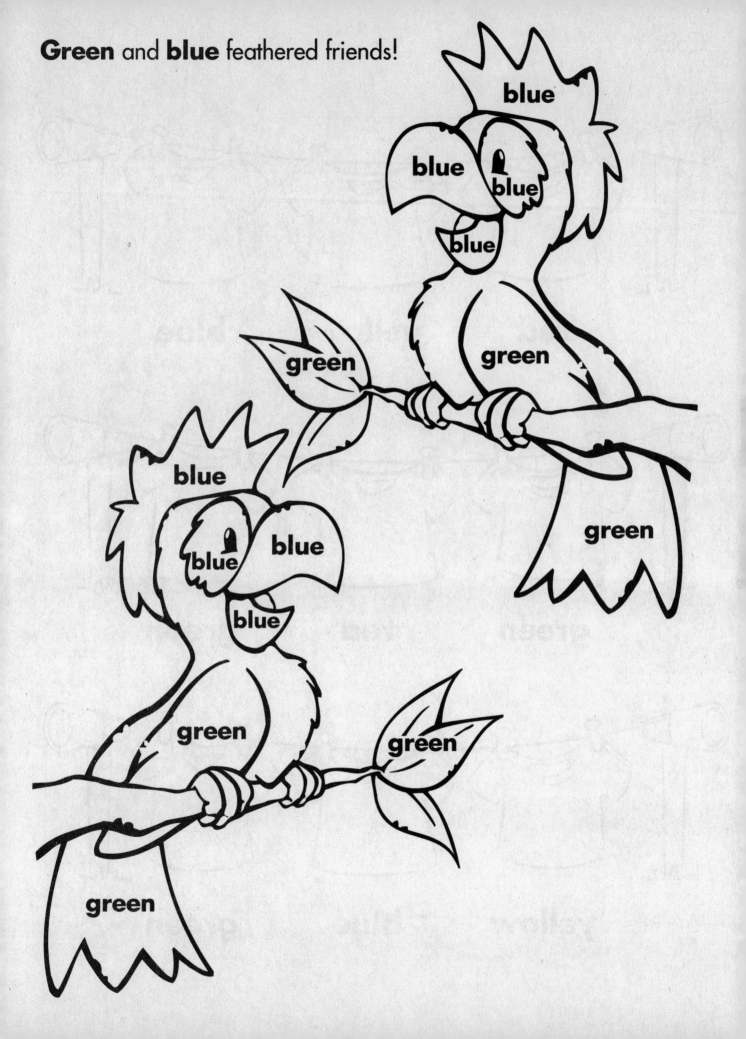

Color.

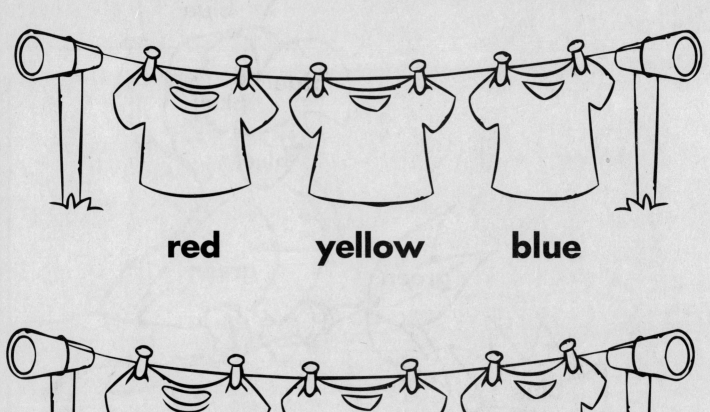

red   **yellow**   **blue**

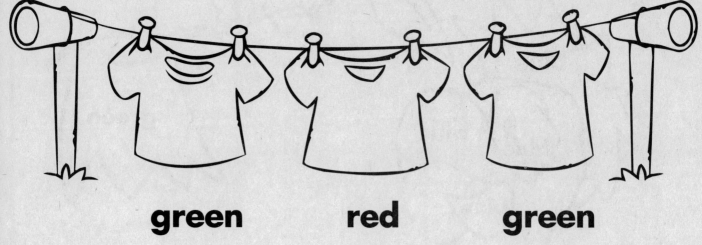

green   **red**   **green**

yellow   **blue**   **green**

Color.

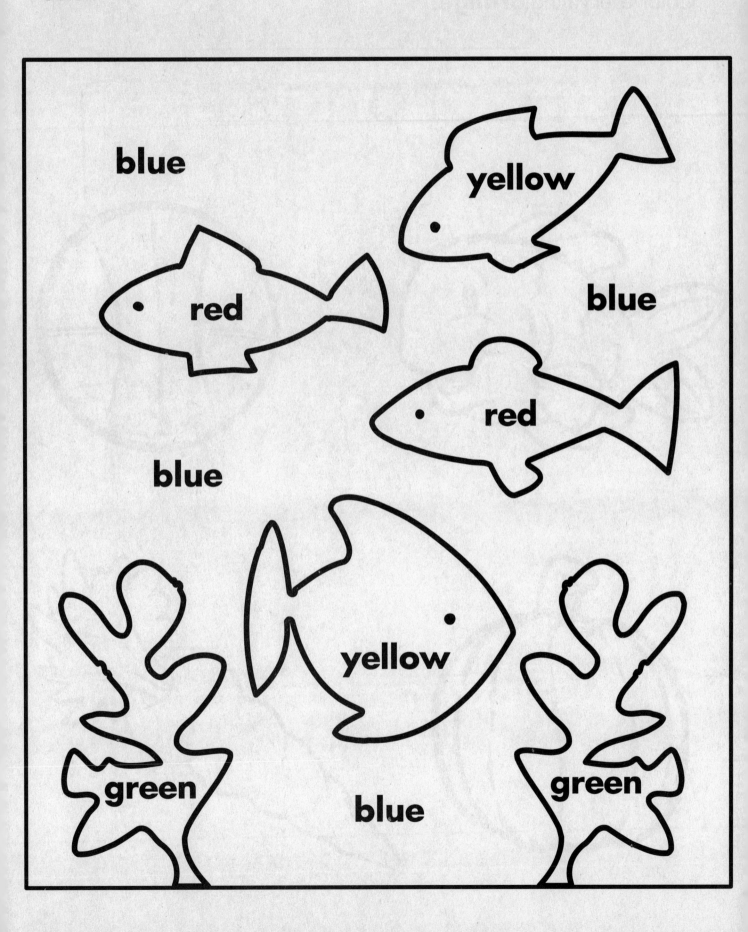

Color everything **orange**.

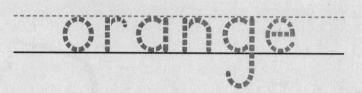

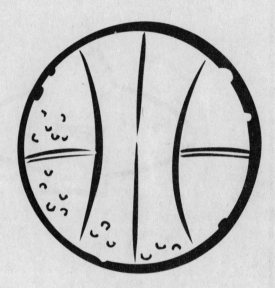

Color everything **black**.

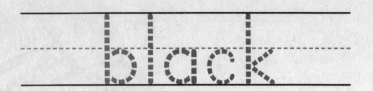

Color everything **purple**.

purple

Color everything **brown**.

brown

Color Key

1 = orange   **2** = brown
3 = black   **4** = purple

Color Key

 s = red

 s = black

 s = purple

 s = blue

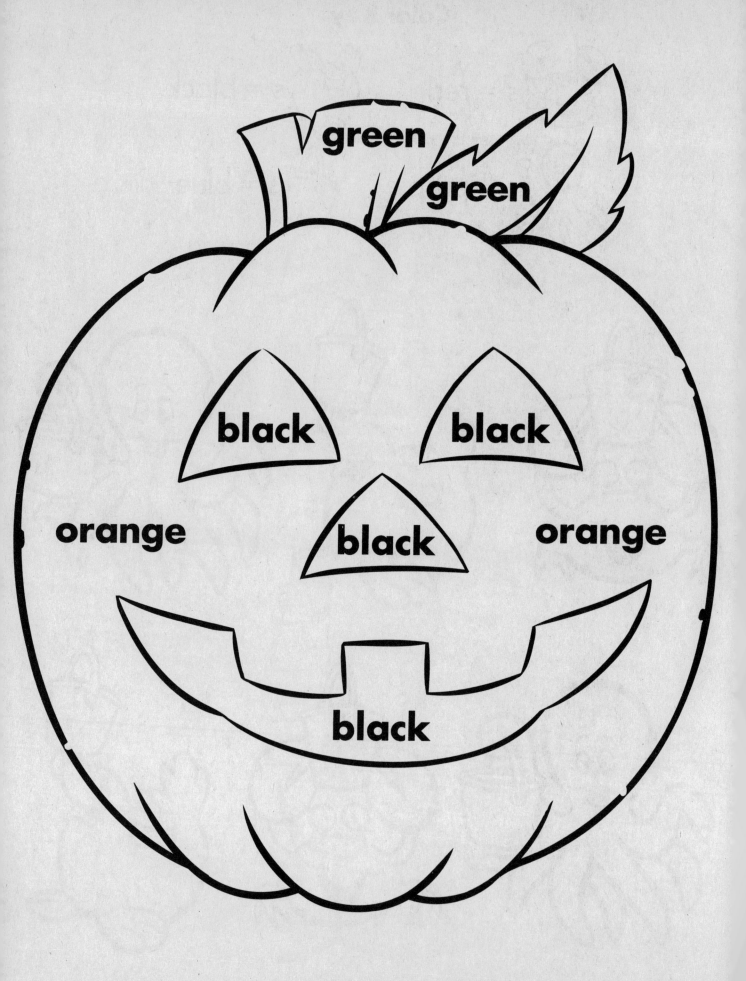

You are a color word champ!
Write your name.
Color the ribbon.

_____
- -
Congratulations _____ **!**

black

orange

blue

COLOR CHAMP!

red

green

brown

yellow

purple

Draw yourself.

Finish drawing the mouse. Color.

What a happy mouse!

Finish drawing the snail. Color.

Such a silly snail!

Finish drawing the train. Color.

Choo-choo!

Color. Circle the animals that do not belong.

Color. Find and circle:

Color. Circle 4 things that are different.

Find and circle 4  s. Color.

Color. Find and circle:

Color. Circle 4 things that are different.

Draw a path to the end of the roller coaster.

STOP

Color. Find and circle:

Color. Circle 4 things that are different.

Draw a path to the water slide.

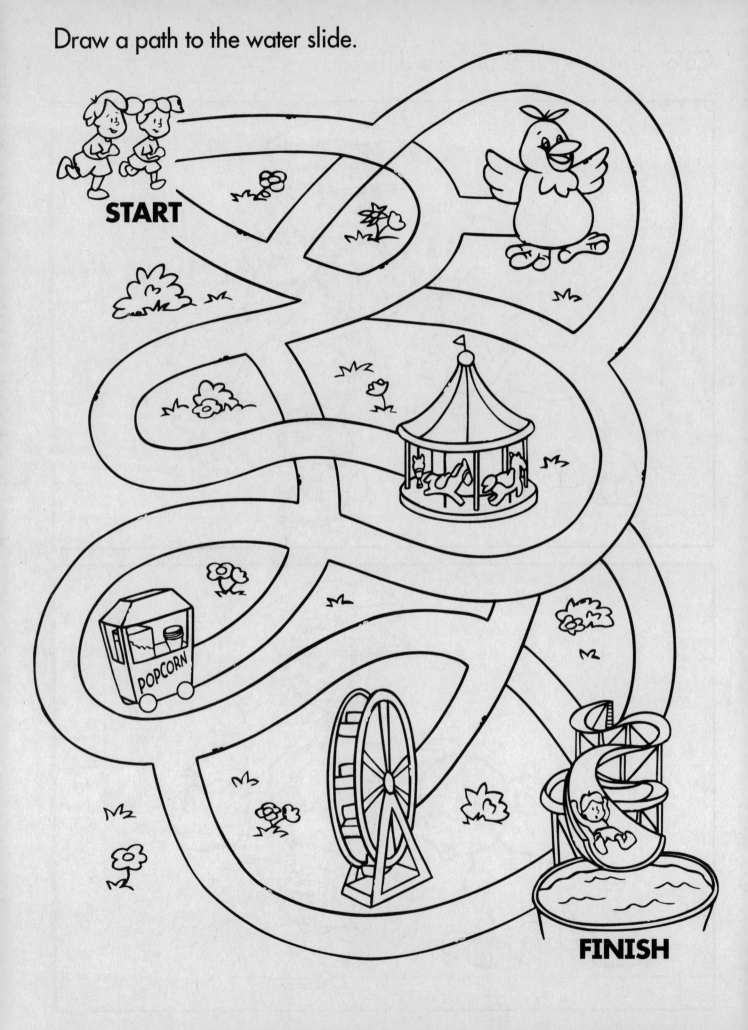

START

POPCORN

FINISH

Color. Circle 5 things that are different.

Color. Find and circle:

Color. Circle what does not belong.

l fish

I horse

Color. Trace **I**.

Alligator plays golf at hole number **I**.

2 rockets

2

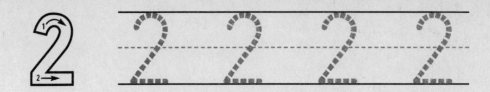

2 planes

Color. Trace **2**.

2 trapeze artists fly!

3

3 skateboards

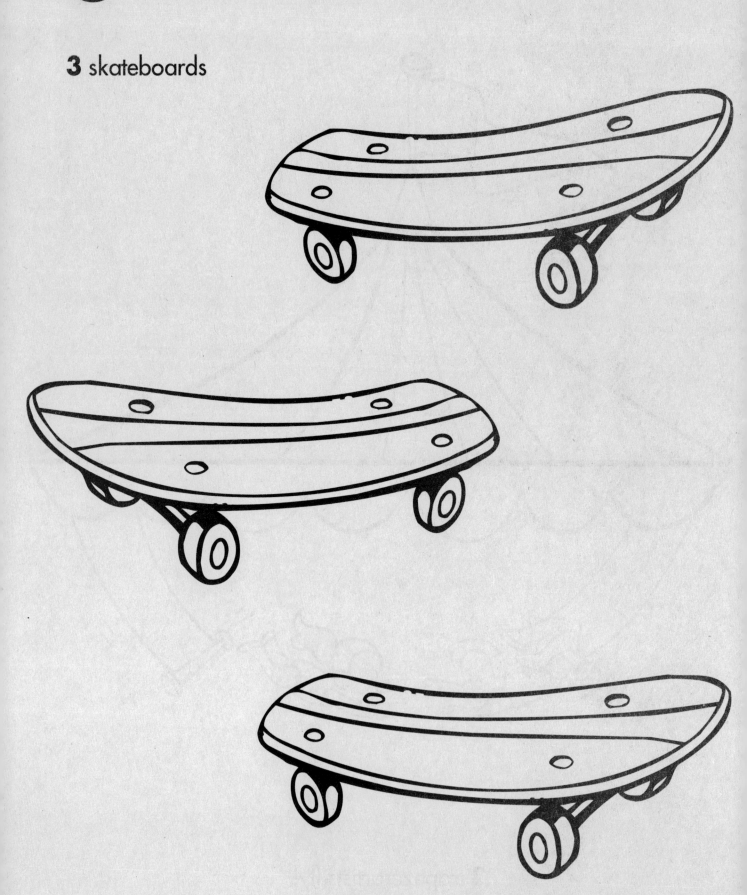

3 3 3 3 3

3 robots

Color. Trace **3**.

3 bouncing balls for you!

Color Key

1 = yellow   **2** = blue   **3** = green

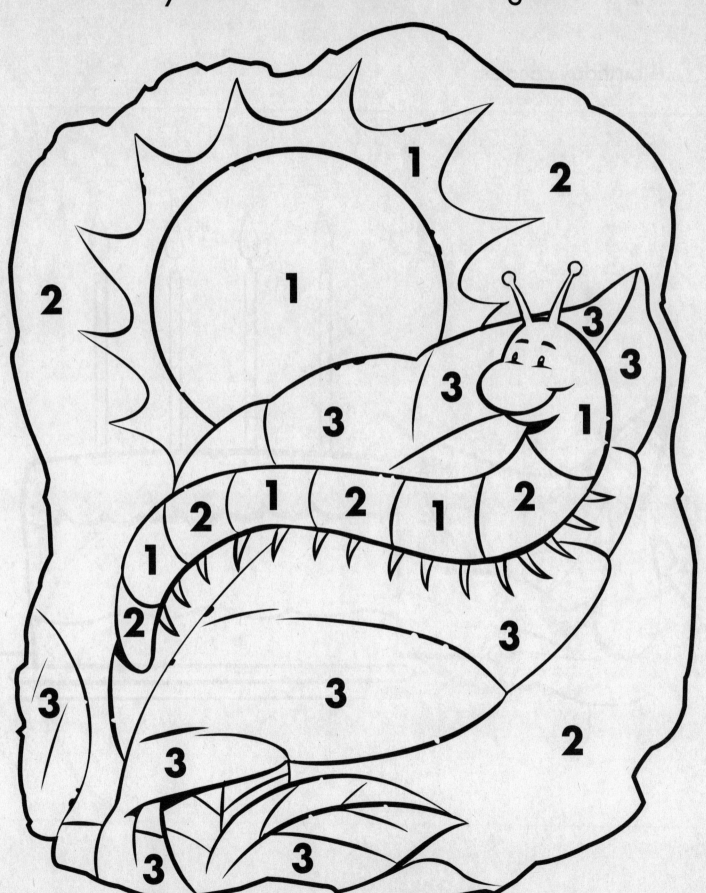

4

4 birthday candles

4

4 balloons

Color. Trace **4**.

4 birthday presents for you!

5 puppy dogs

5

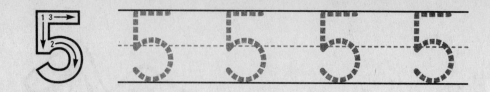

5 kitty cats

Color. Trace **5**.

5 pretty parrots want crackers!

Color Key

1 = brown   **2** = orange   **3** = blue
4 = yellow   **5** = green

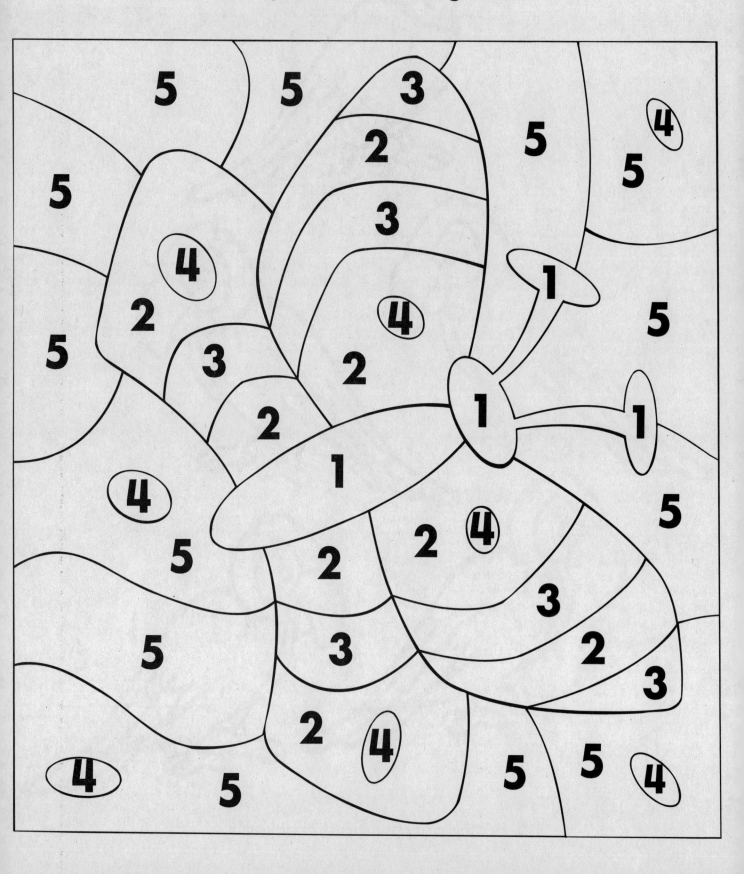

Connect the dots from **1** to **5**. Color.

6

6 bugs

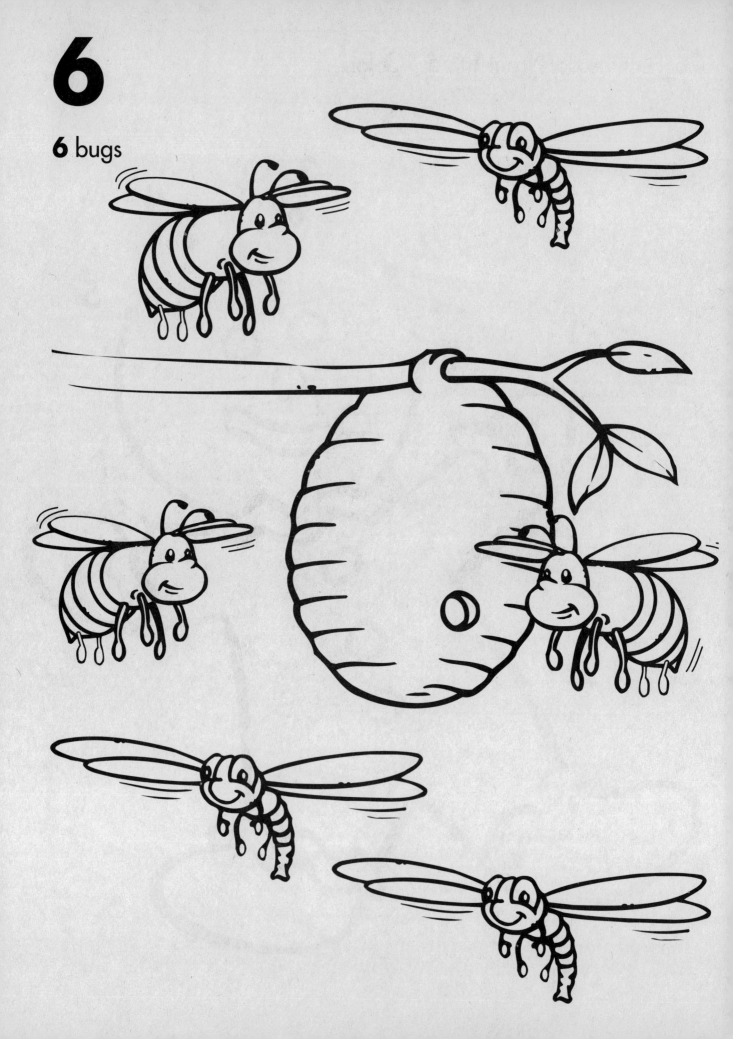

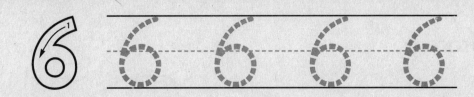

6 hummingbirds

Color. Trace **6**.

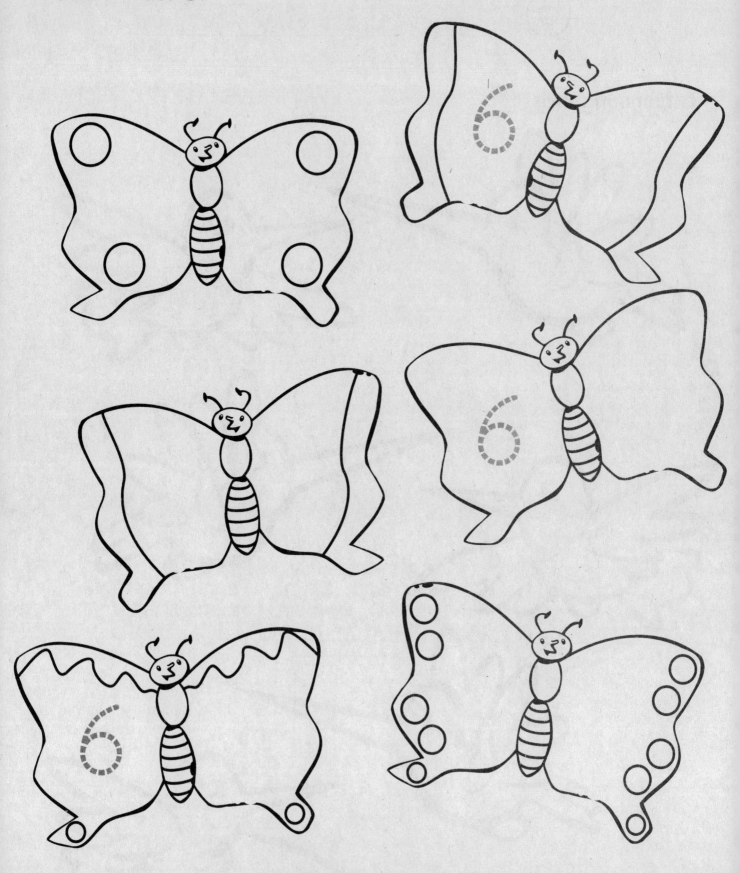

6 butterflies fly in the air.

Color Key

1 = green   **2** = purple   **3** = brown
4 = blue   **5** = orange   **5** = yellow

7

7 blocks

7 turtles

Color. Trace **7**.

7 cupcakes make a yummy treat!

8 chickens go for a ride.

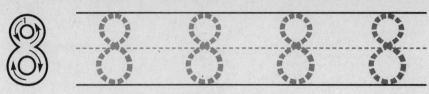

8 ducks

Color. Trace **8**.

8 happy pigs live on a farm.

9

9 daffodils

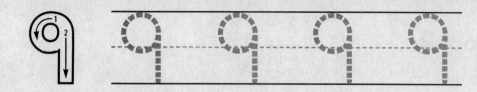

9 daisies

Color. Trace **9**.

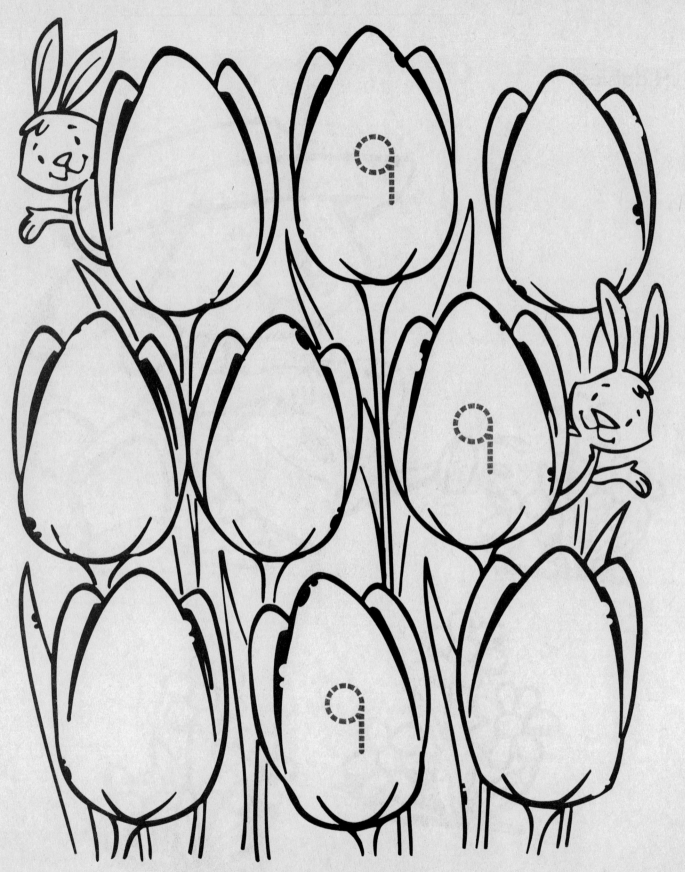

9 spring tulips grow.

Connect the dots from 1 to 9.

10

10 fancy eggs

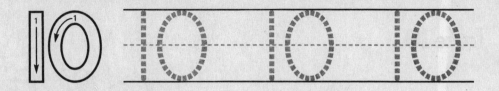

10 chickadees

Color. Trace **10**.

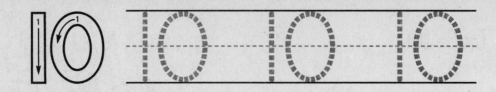

10 chickadees

Connect the dots from **1** to **10**.

Follow the path from 1 to 10.

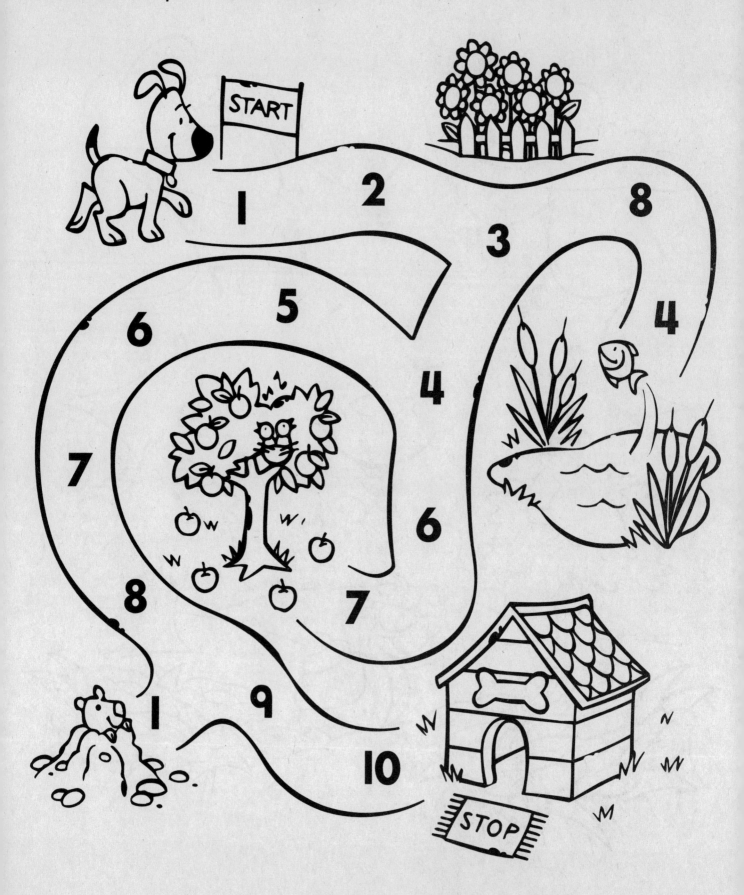

Connect the dots from **1** to **10**.

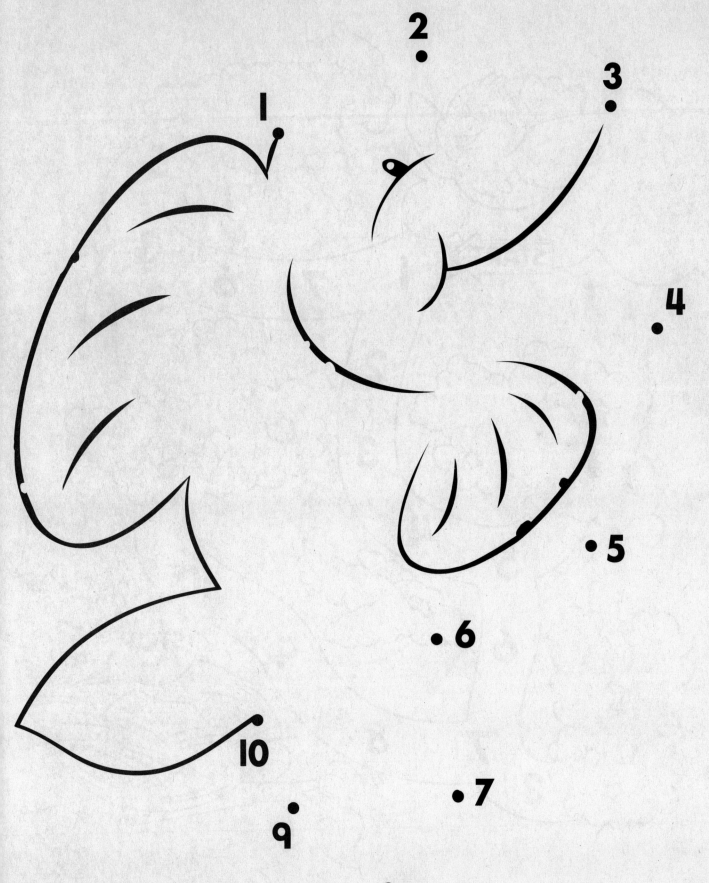

Follow the path from **1** to **10**.

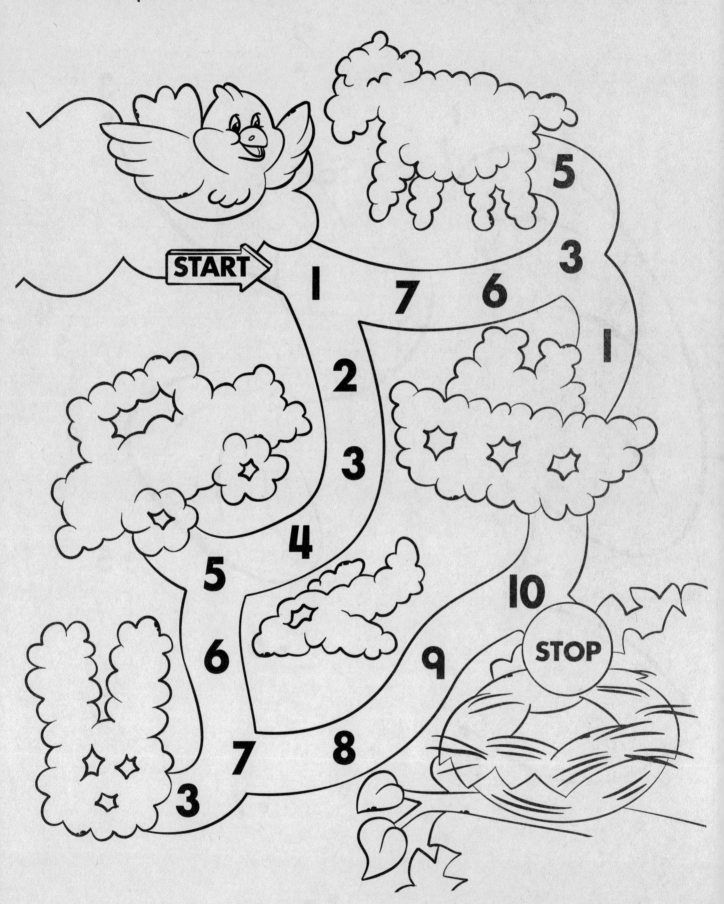

Find the hidden numbers **1** to **10**.

1 2 3 4 5 6 7 8 9 10

Connect the dots from **1** to **10**.

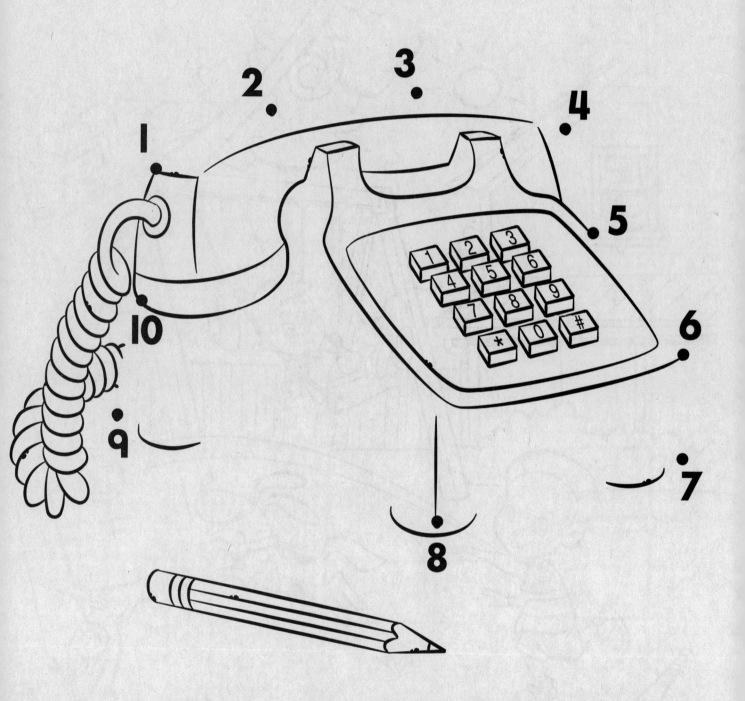

Follow the path from **1** to **10**.

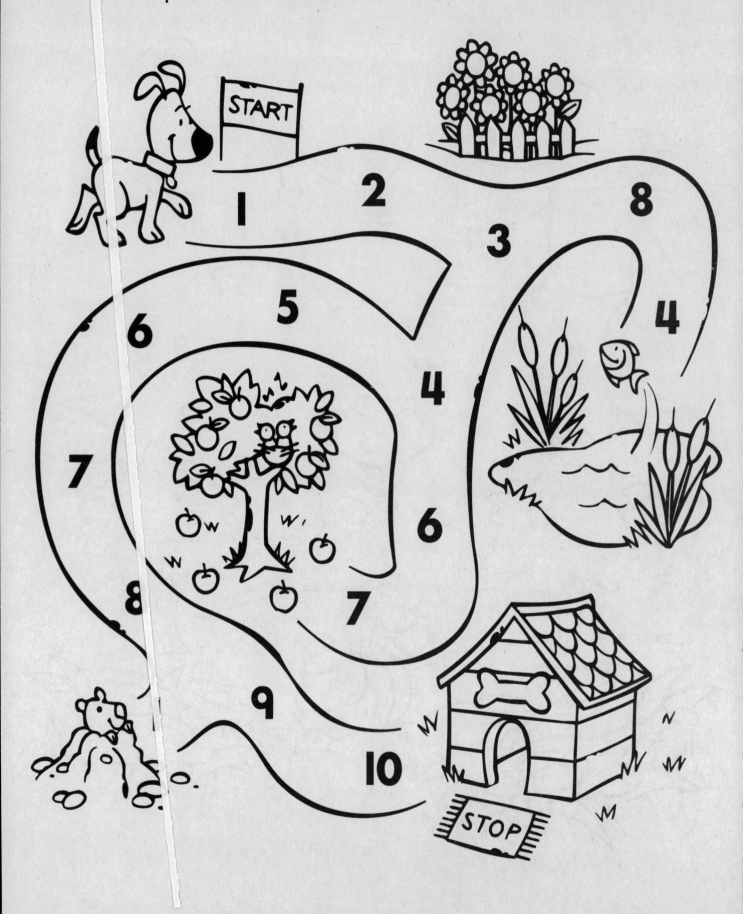

Follow the path from **1** to **10**.

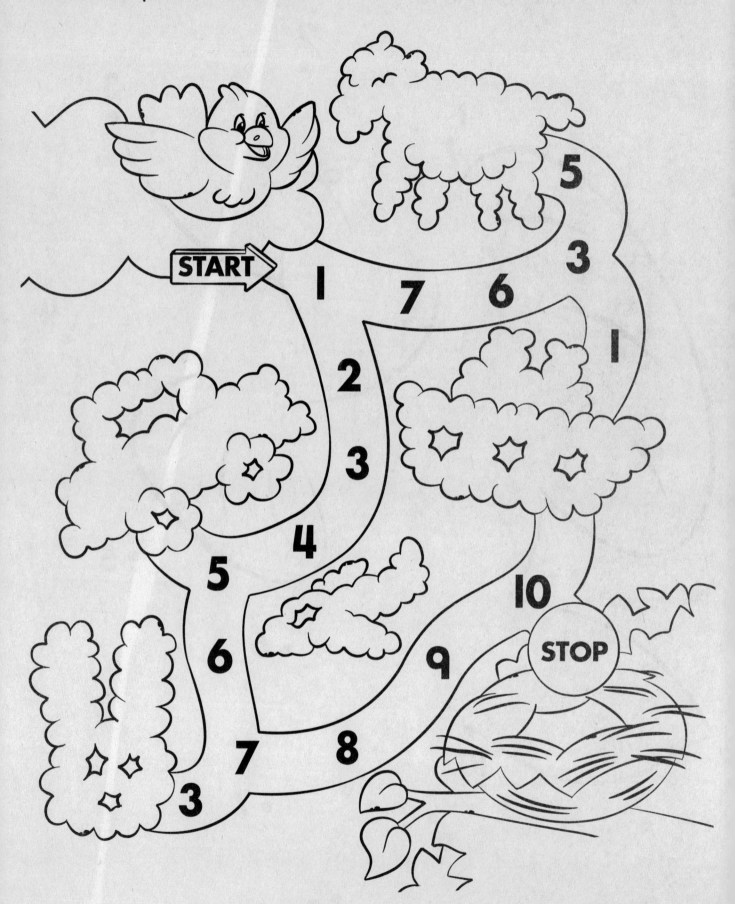

Connect the dots from **1** to **10**.

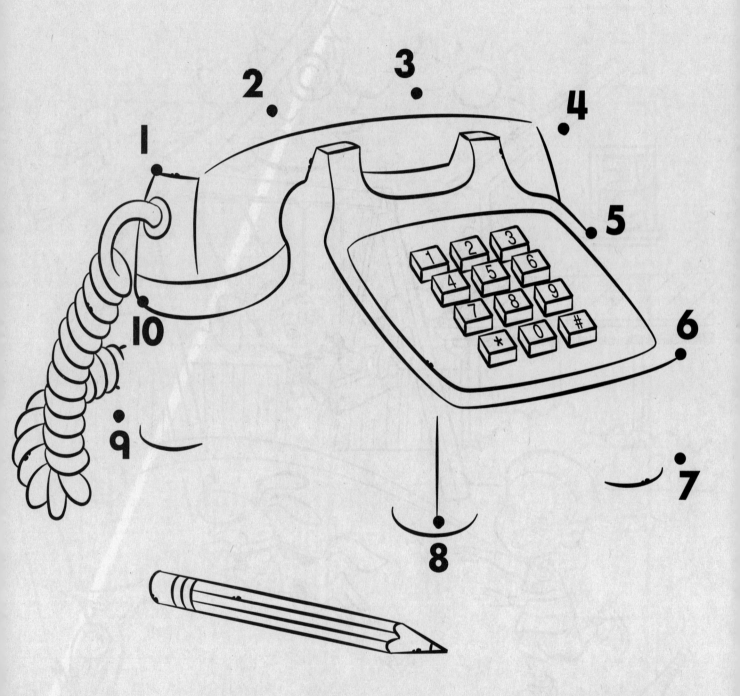

Find the hidden numbers **1** to **10**.

1 2 3 4 5 6 7 8 9 10

Connect the dots from 1 to 10.

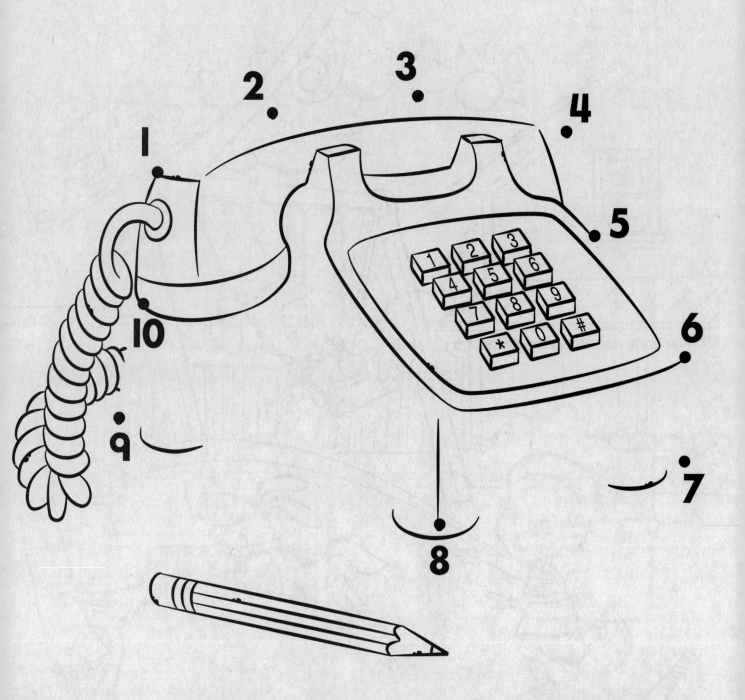

Fill in the missing numbers from **1** to **10**.

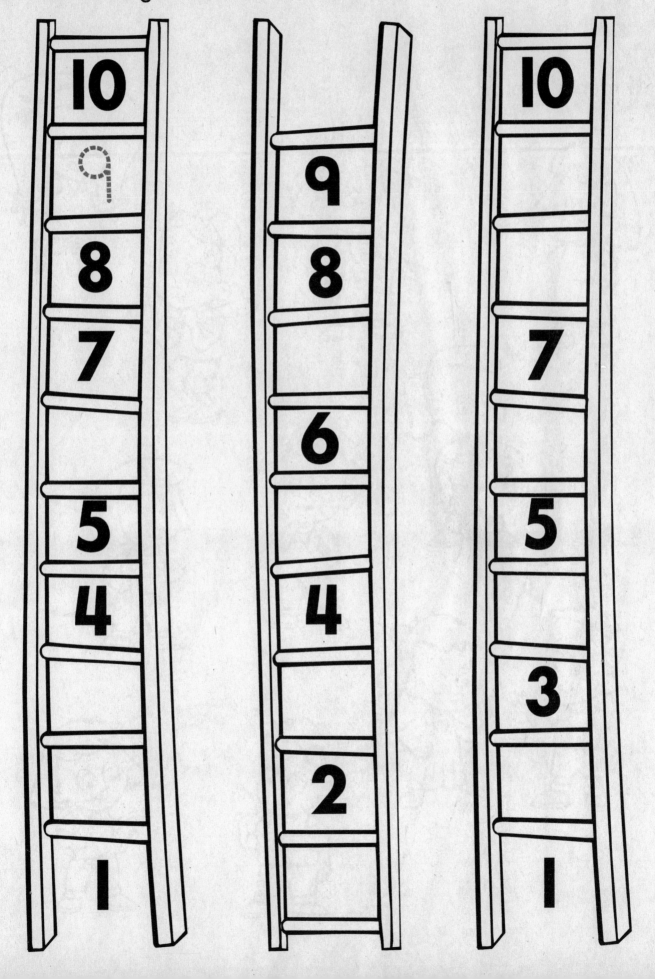

11 friends at play!

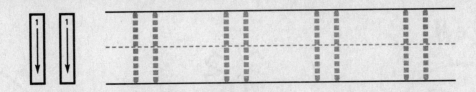

II people in the city.

Color. Trace **ll**.

ll hats

12 more leaves left to rake up!

12

12 12 12

12 trees

Color. Trace **12**.

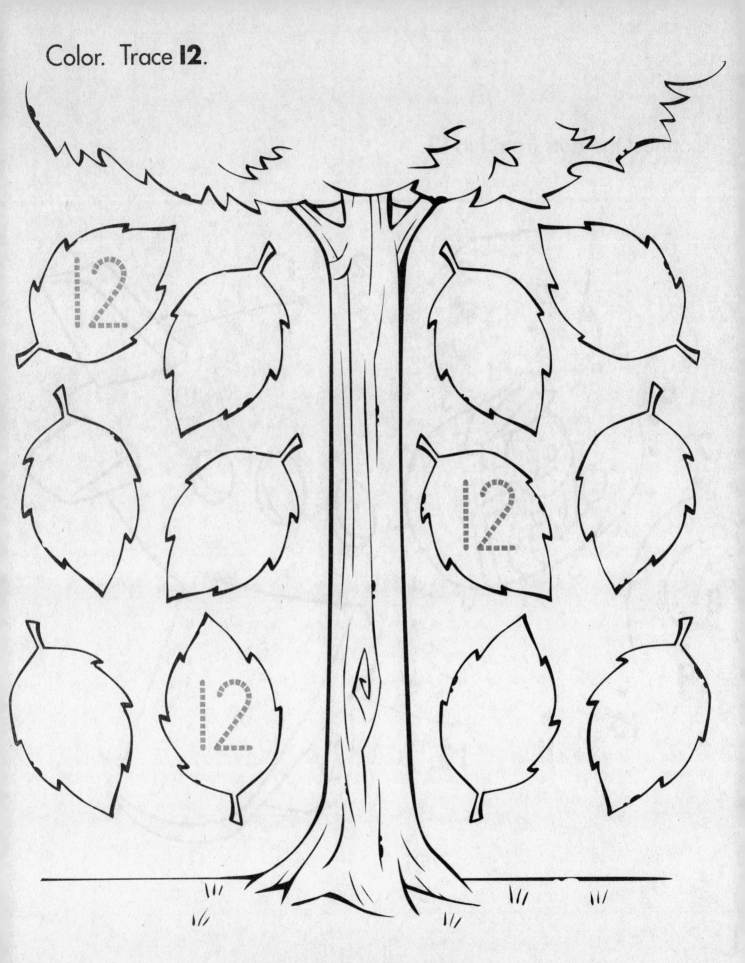

12 leaves are falling down.

Connect the dots from **1** to **12**.

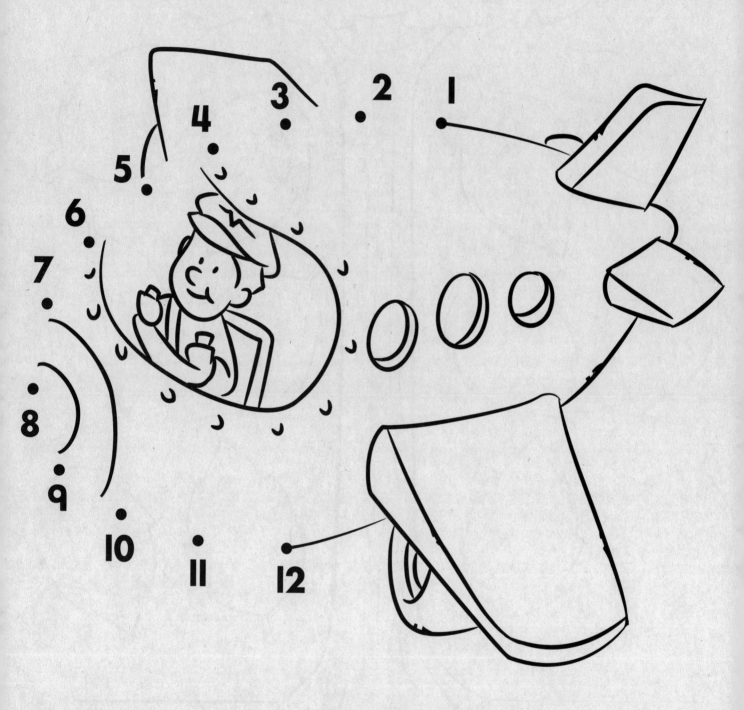

Find **12**  s. Color.

Follow the path from **1** to **12**.

13 seashells

13

13

13 13 13 13

13 sea creatures swim in the ocean.

Color. Trace **13**.

14

14 crayons

14

14 school tools

Color. Trace **14**.

Alligator artists love to paint **14**!

Color Key

10 = yellow   **11** = red   **12** = blue
13 = green   **14** = orange

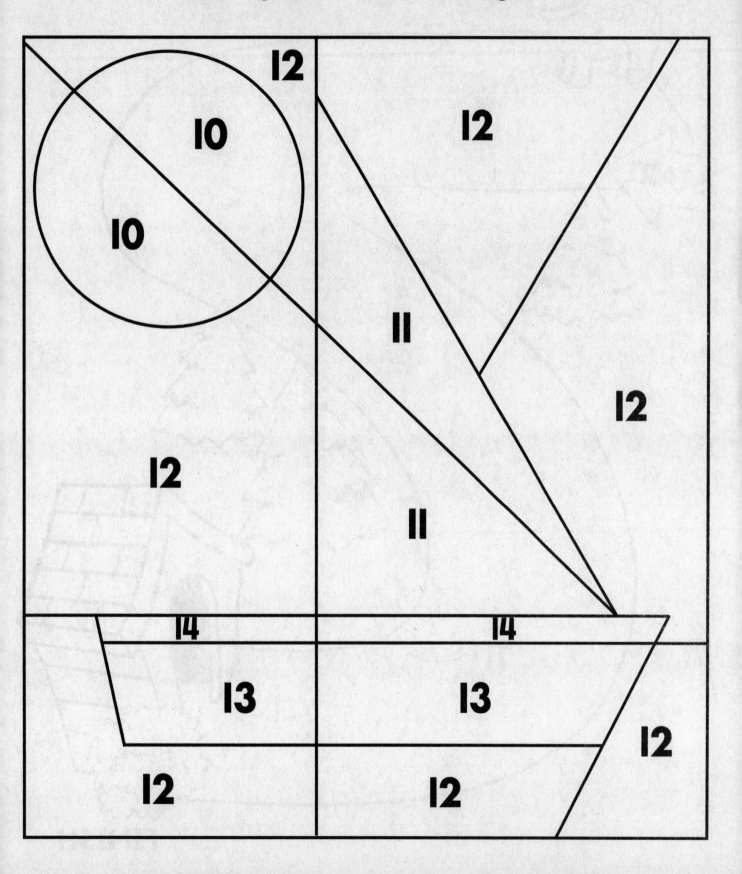

Trace **8** to **14** then draw a line to follow the path.

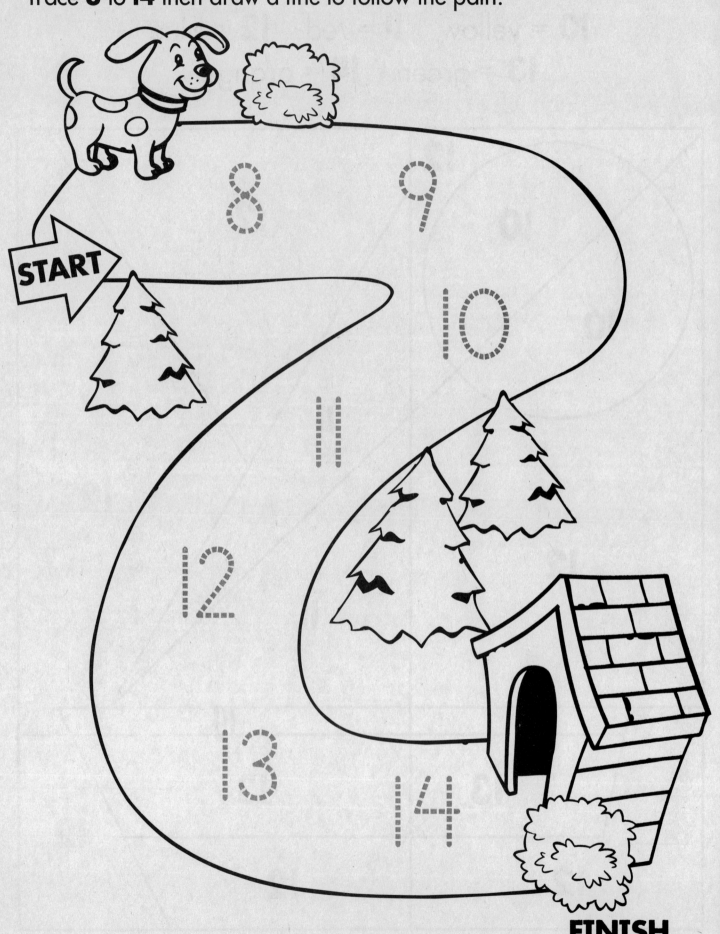

START

8

9

10

11

12

13

14

FINISH

Connect the dots from **1** to **14**.

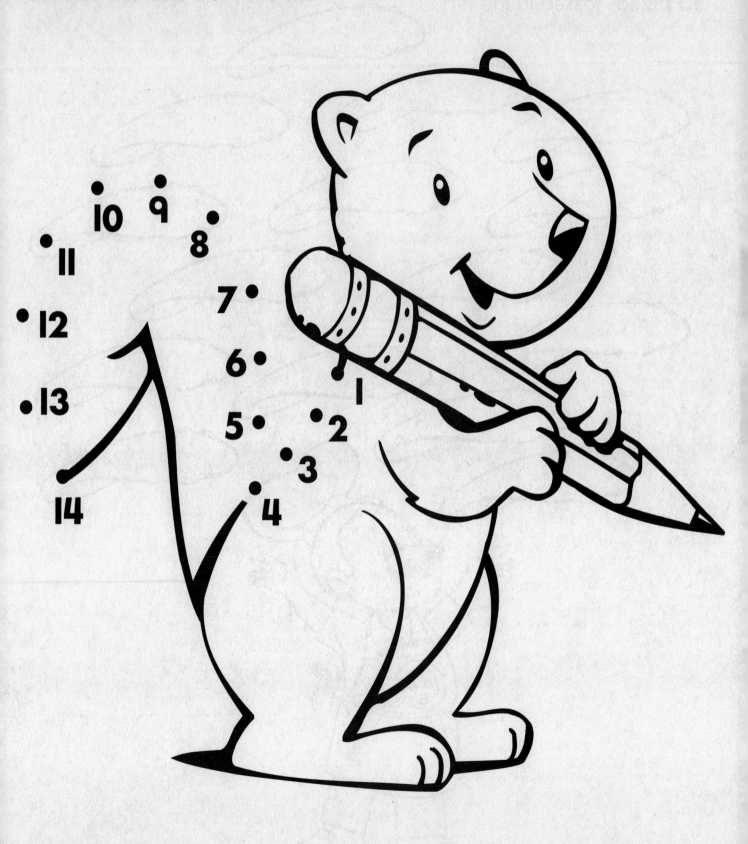

15

15 pizzas tossed in the air!

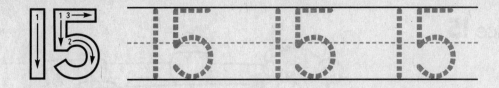

15 pancakes flipped in the air!

Color. Trace 15.

Betty Bear baked **15** cookies!

Connect the dots from **1** to **15**.

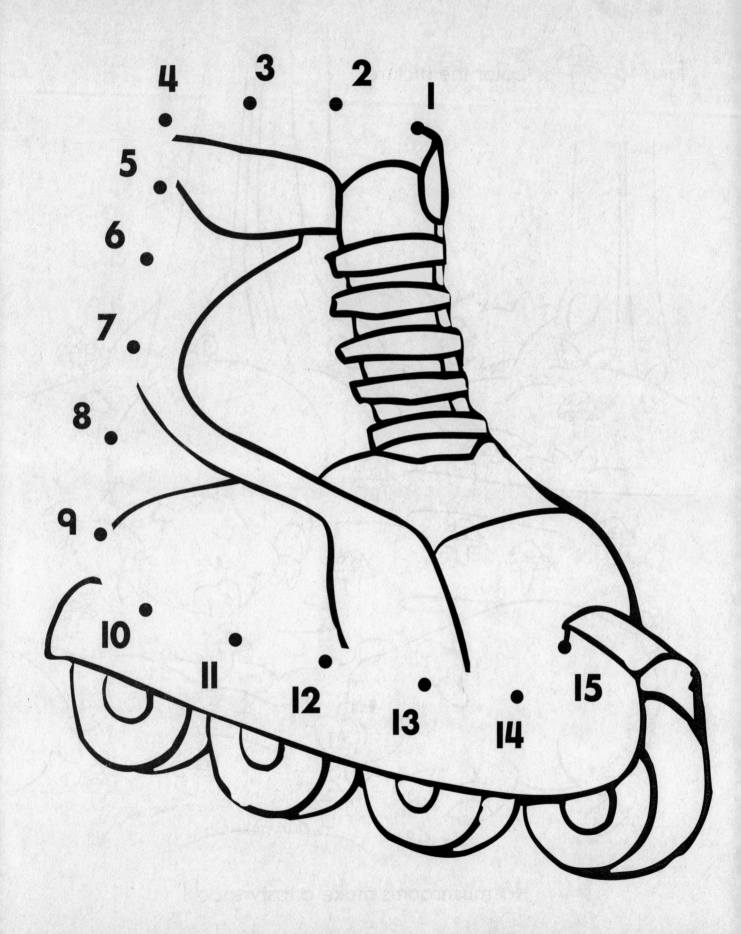

16

Find **16** s. Color the picture.

16 mushrooms make a tasty snack!

16 16 16 16

16 stars shine in the sky.

Color. Trace **16**.

Connect the dots from **1** to **16**.

Draw a path from **1** to **16** to help the boy get home.

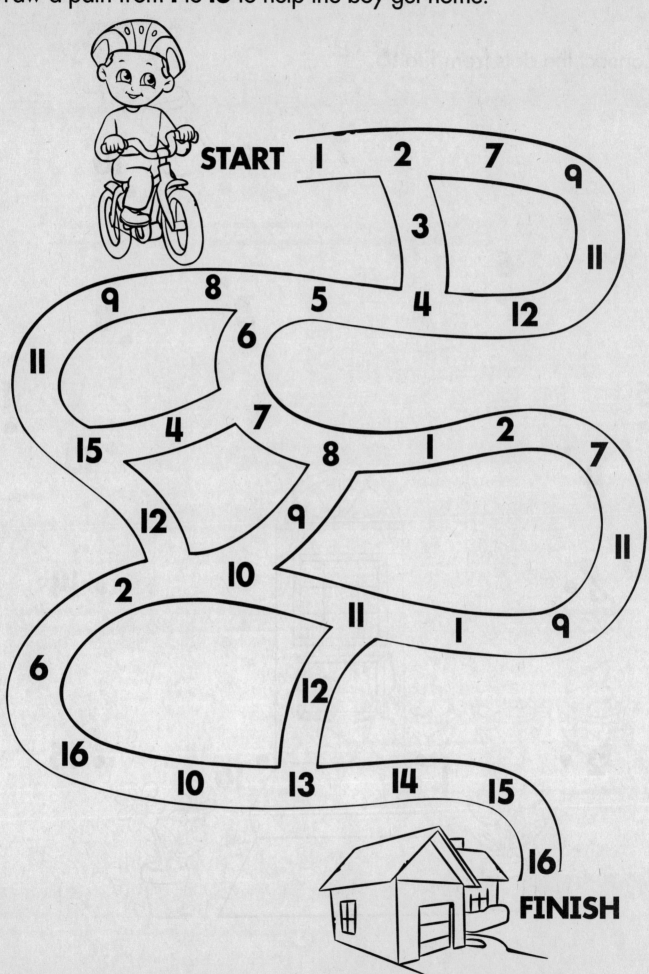

17 toys

17 17 17 17 17

Can you see **17** balls in the toy store window?

Color. Trace **17**.

18

18 apples grow on an apple tree.

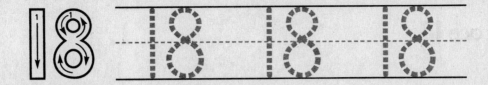

18 apples in baskets

Color. Trace **18**.

Draw a path from **1** to **18**.

19

19 ice cream treats

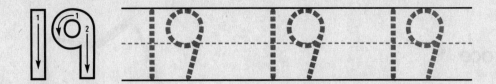

Look! **19** great big gumballs!

Color. Trace **19**.

Draw a path from **1** to **19**.

20

20 snowflakes

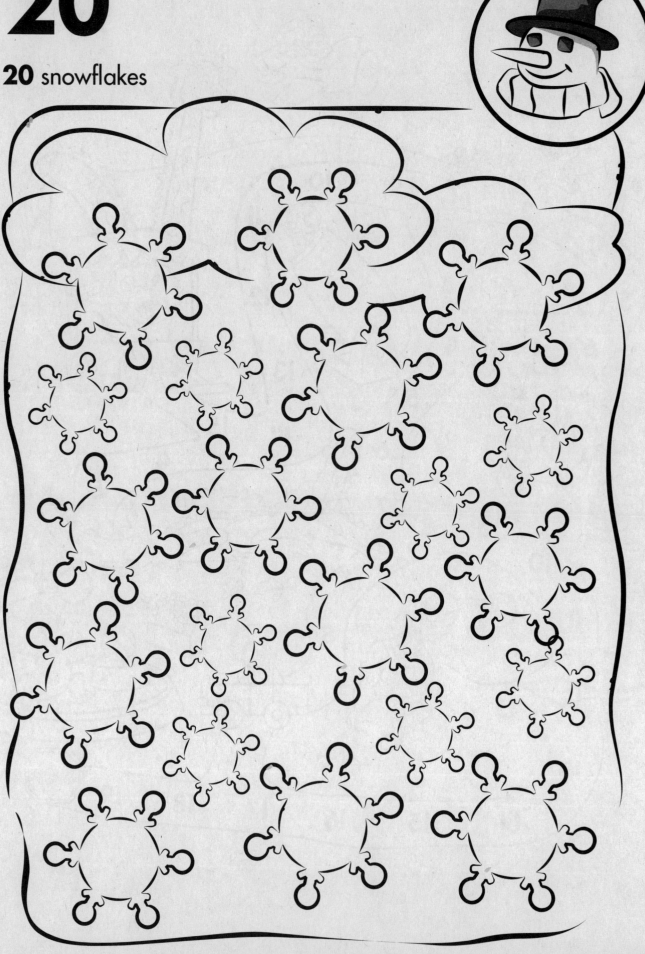

20 20 20 20

20 snowballs

Color. Trace **20**.

First connect the dots from **1** to **11**.
Then connect the dots from **12** to **20**.

Follow the path from **I** to **20**.

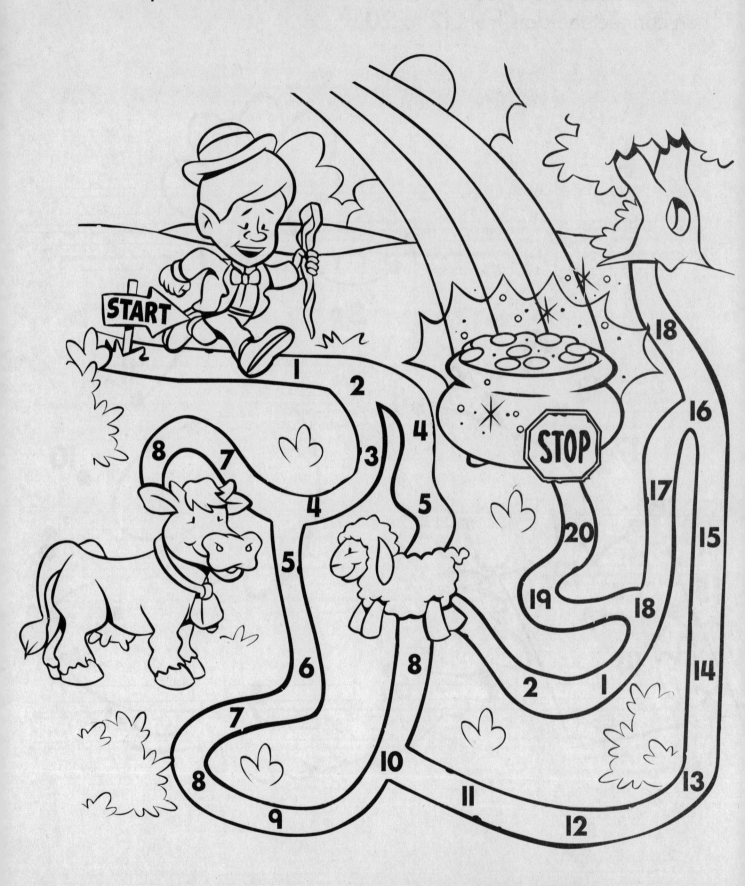

Trace. Write the missing numbers. Color the train.

Color Key

16 = yellow   **17** = blue   **18** = red
19 = green   **20** = brown

Connect the dots from **8** to **20**.

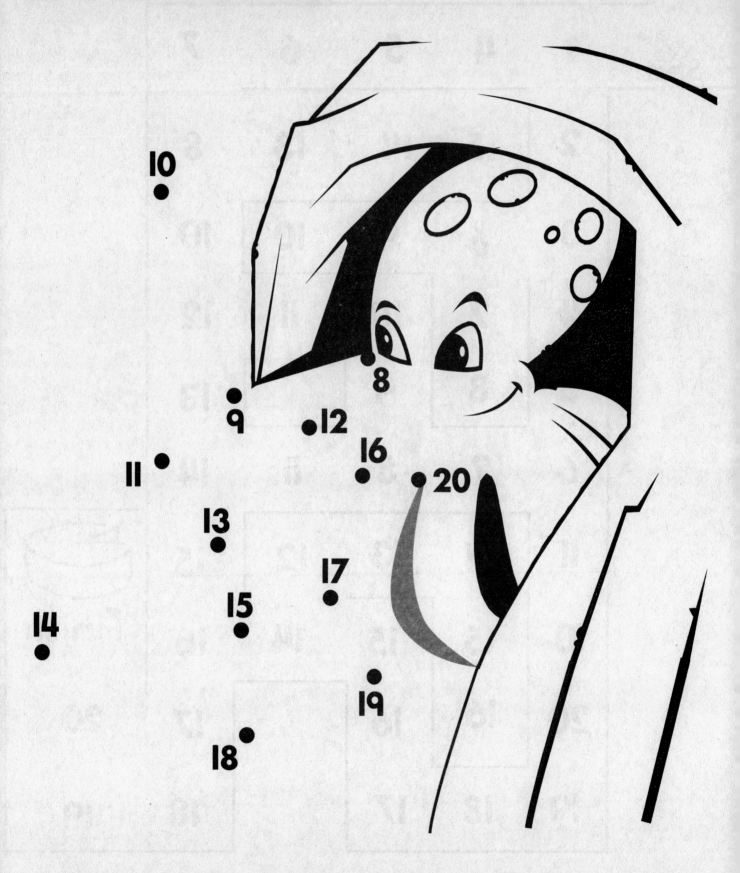

Follow the path from **1** to **20**.

Start

1	4	5	6	7
2	15	14	13	8
3	6	9	10	10
4	7	10	11	12
5	8	9		13
6	7	8	11	14
11	14	13	12	15
10	15	15	14	16
20	16	16		17
19	18	17	18	19

Finish

20

Connect the dots from **1** to **20**.

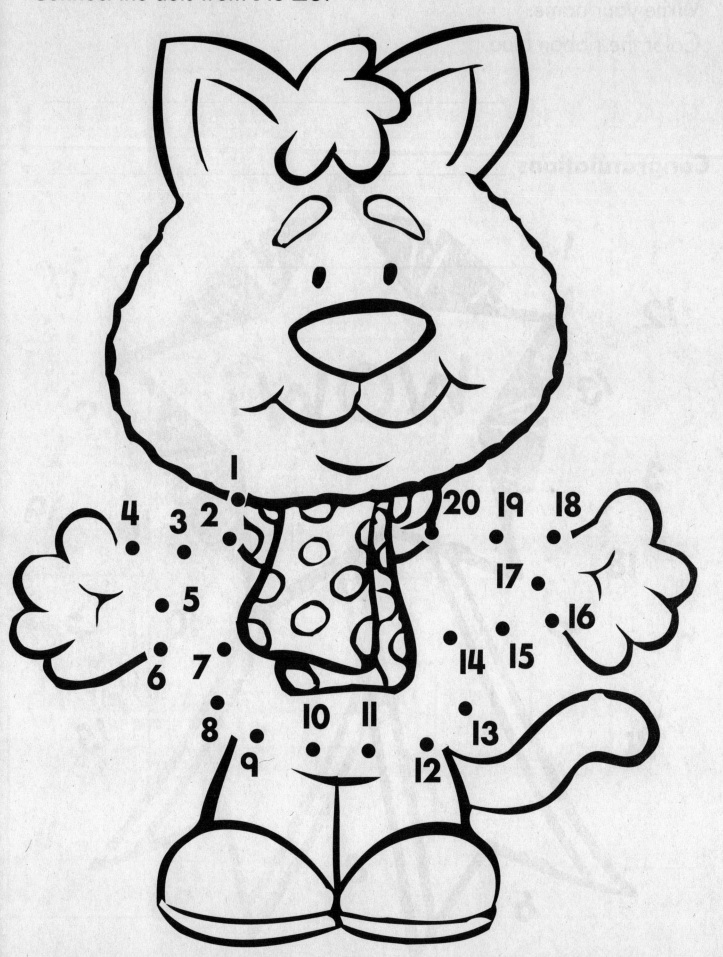

Hooray! You know the numbers **1** to **20**!
Write your name.
Color the ribbon blue.

_____

Congratulations _____ **!**

1 one

One cake

2 two

Two cupcakes

3 three

three

Three frosted brownies

4 four

Four candy canes

5 five

five

Five cookies

6 six

Six ice cream cones

7 seven

Seven lollipops

8 eight

Eight cherries

9 nine

Nine ice pops

10 ten

Ten candies

_____

one

One backpack

Two boys swing!

three

Three mice like to roller skate!

four

Four monkeys swing in the air!

five

Kitty chases **five** squirrels!

Color Key

one = blue   **two** = orange   **three** = green

four = red   **five** = yellow

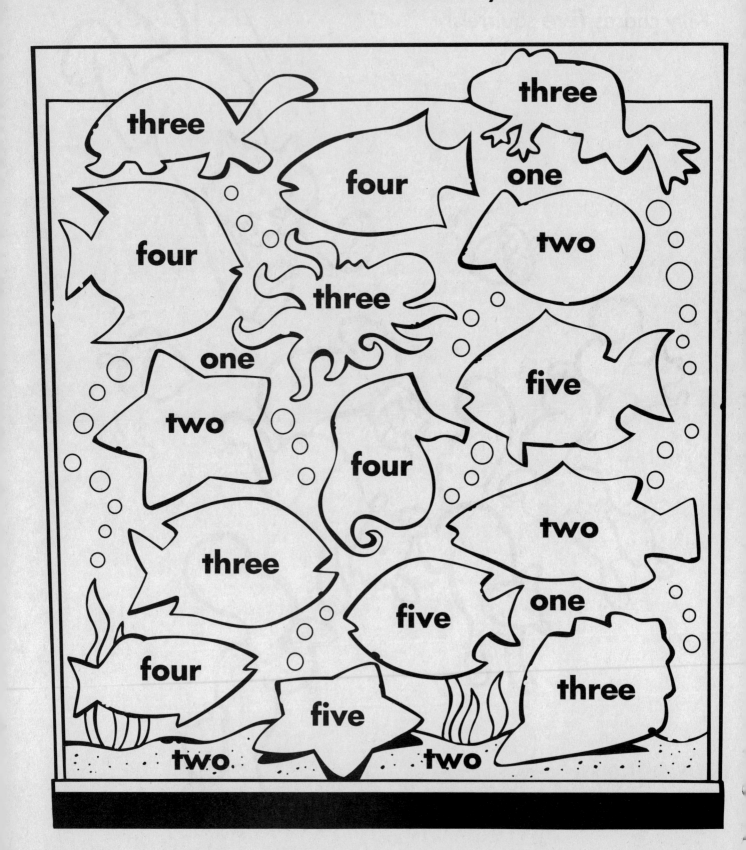

Circle the number words in the puzzle.

n m f i v e

t h r e e p

i g h o n e

x f o u r b

z t w o t o

one   two   three

four   five

six

Six friends play at the park.

seven

Bob counts **seven** sheep to fall asleep!

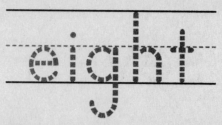

eight

Alligator blows out **eight** candles on his cake!

nine

The piggy bank holds **nine** cents.

ten

Peg and Ed have **ten** blocks.

Color Key

six = orange   **seven** = yellow
eight = green   **nine** = blue   **ten** = red

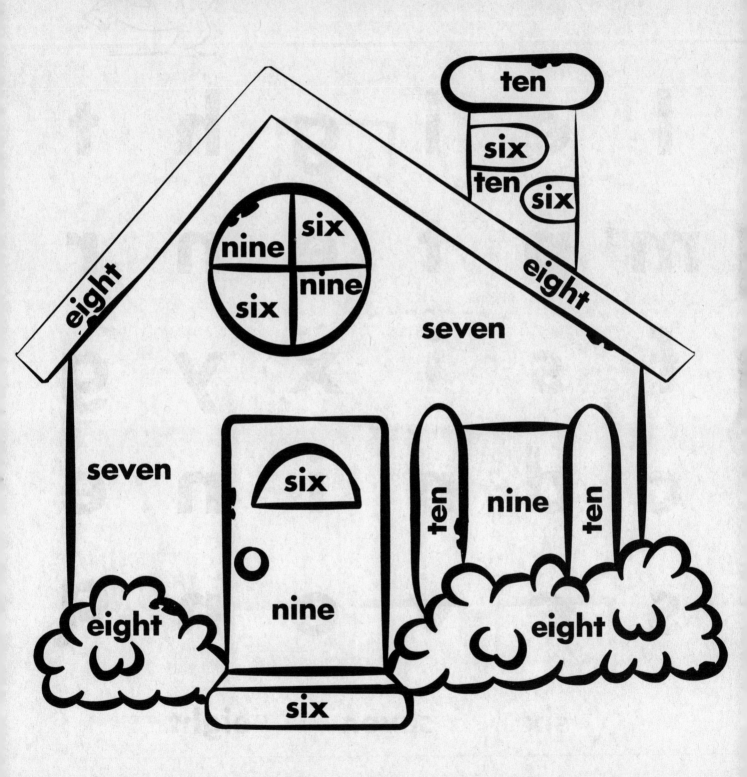

Circle the number words in the puzzle.

l e i g h t
m p t e n r
f s i x y g
c d n i n e
s e v e n q

six   seven   eight

nine   ten

Follow the path from **one** to **ten**.

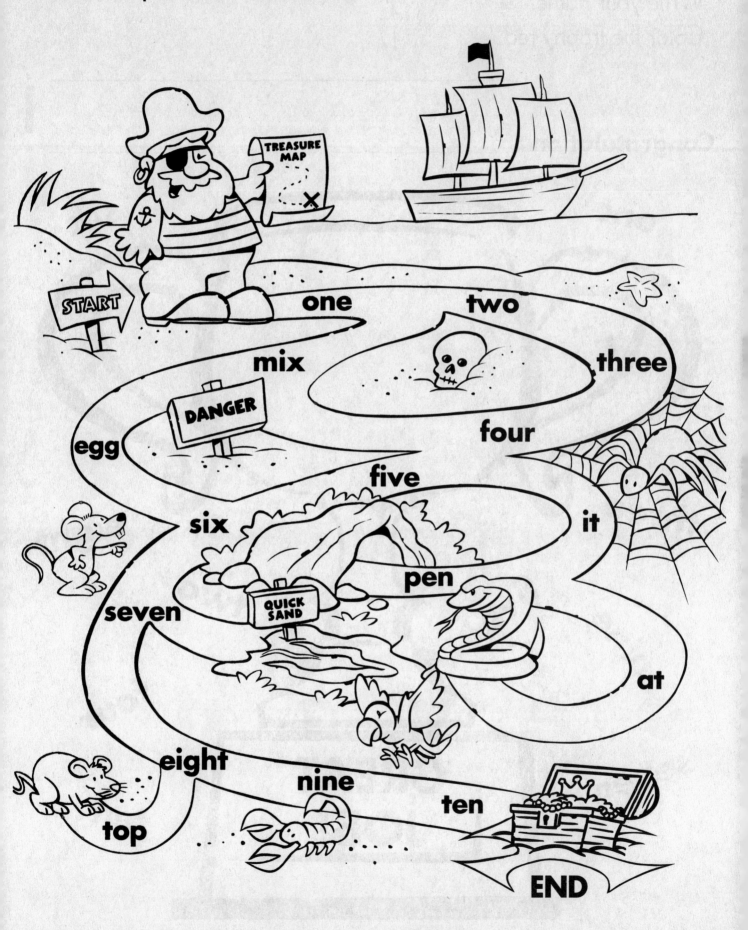

You are a number word champ!
Write your name.
Color the trophy red.

_____ **!**

Congratulations _____ **!**

one
six
three
eight
nine
five
two
four
seven
ten

GREAT
JOB!

1

2

3

4

2 two

1 one

4 four

3 three

5

6

7

8

6 six

5 five

8 eight

7 seven

9

10

11

12

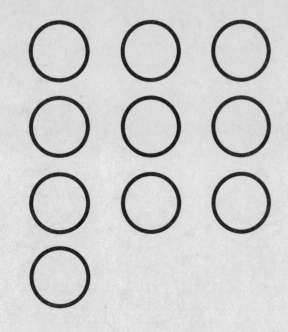

10 ten

9 nine

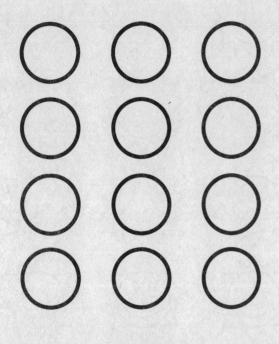

12

11

13

14

15

16

14

13

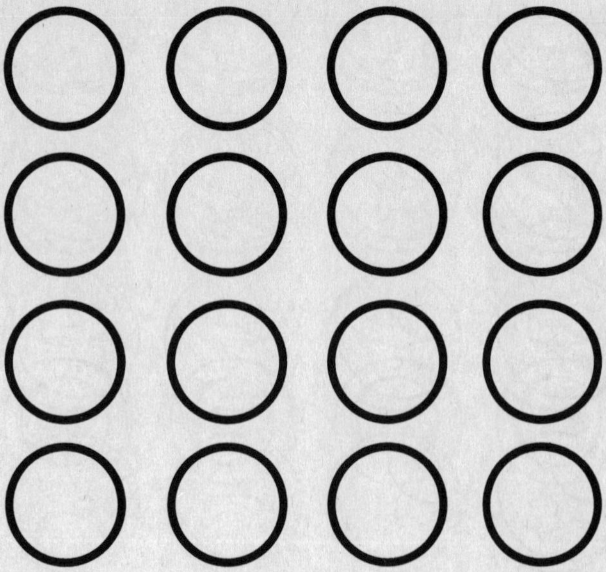

16

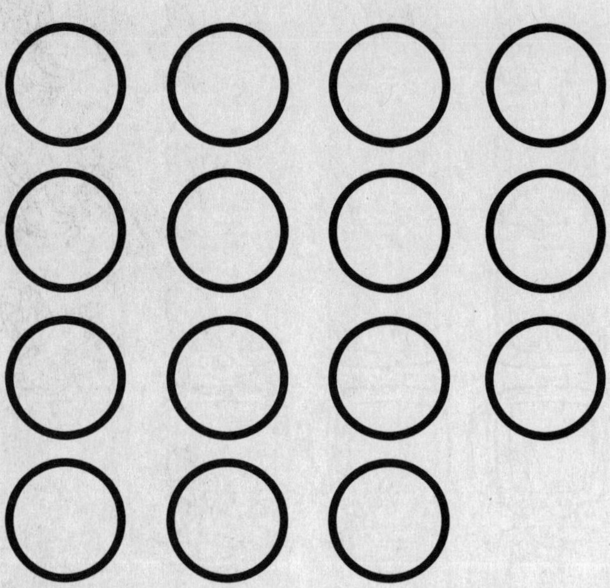

15

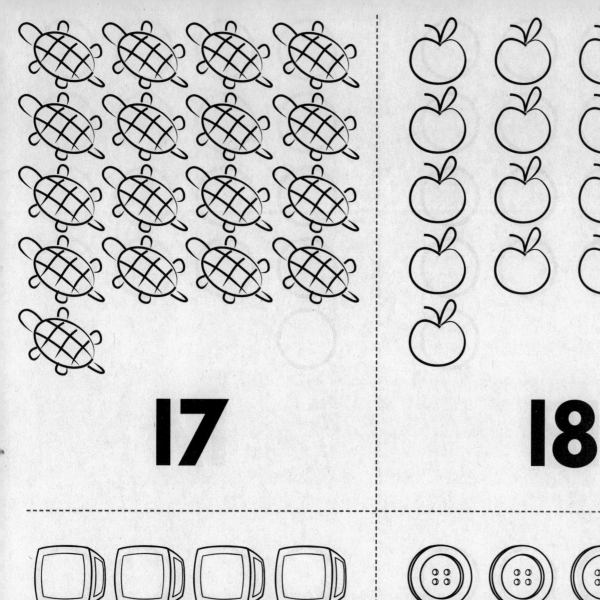

17

18

19

20

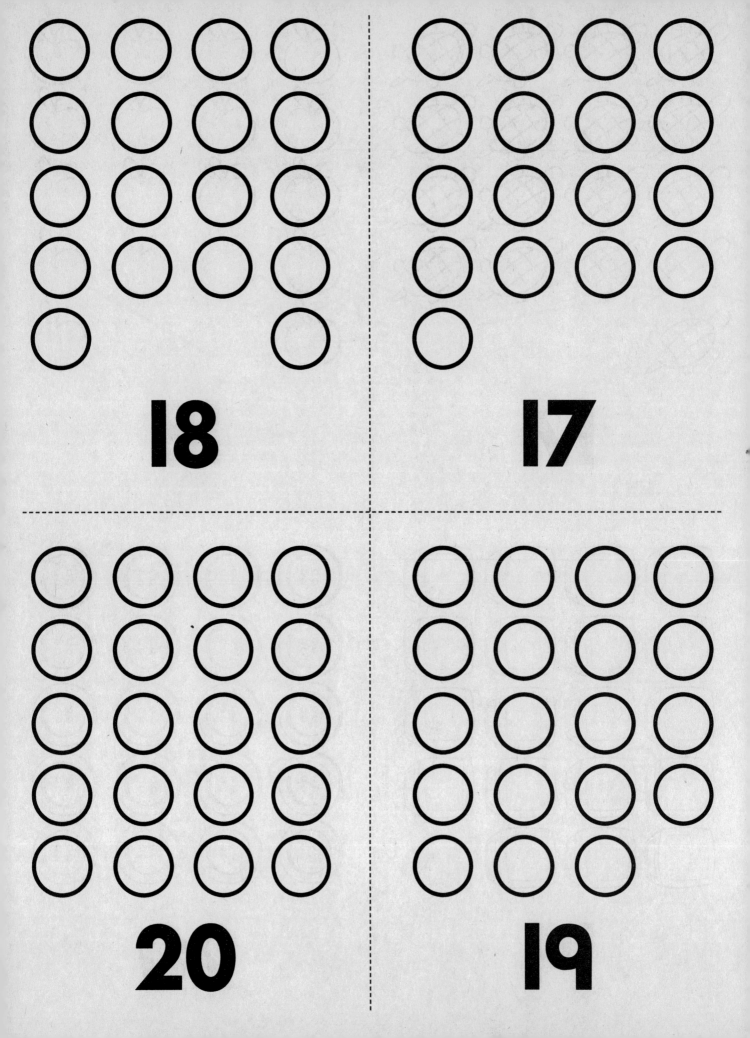

Count. Circle the number of each pet.

3 4

3 4

4 5

4 5

4 5

2 3

Count. Match.

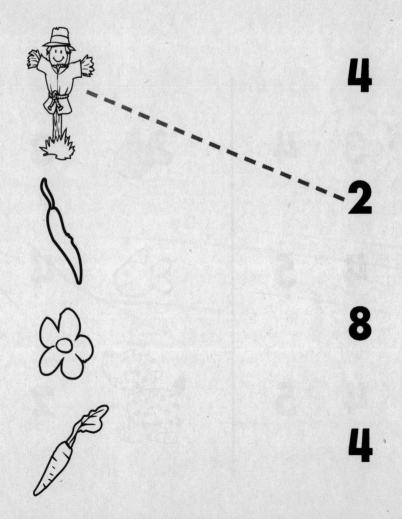

4

2

8

4

Find 15 creatures in the forest!

Color. Count.

Color. Count. What's different?

Color. Count each kind of animal.

Count. Write how many.

How many s? _____

How many s? _____

How many s? _____

How many s? _____

Find The Mice!

Count 9 mice!
Sleep tight, mice!

Mice like to hide!
Find the mice!

Find 3 mice!

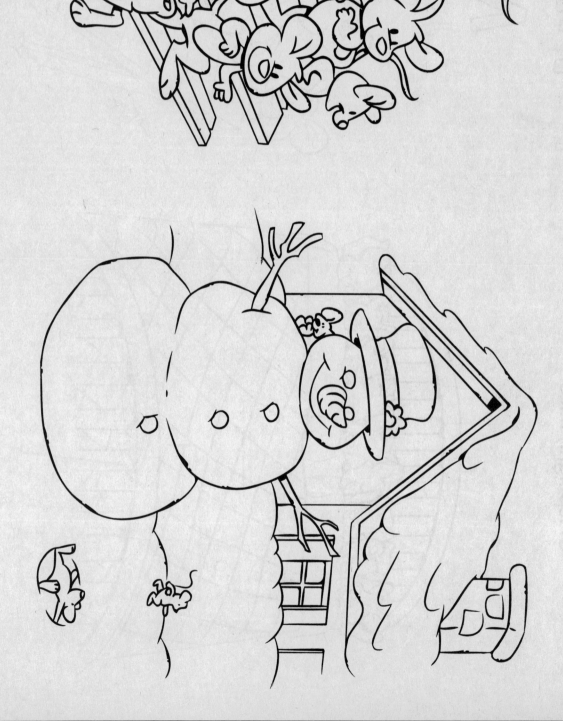

Find 5 mice!

Find 3 mice!

4

Find 3 mice!

Find 9 mice!

5

Finish drawing the teddy bear, then color.

Teddy's pockets and straps are **rectangles**!

Finish drawing the house, then color.

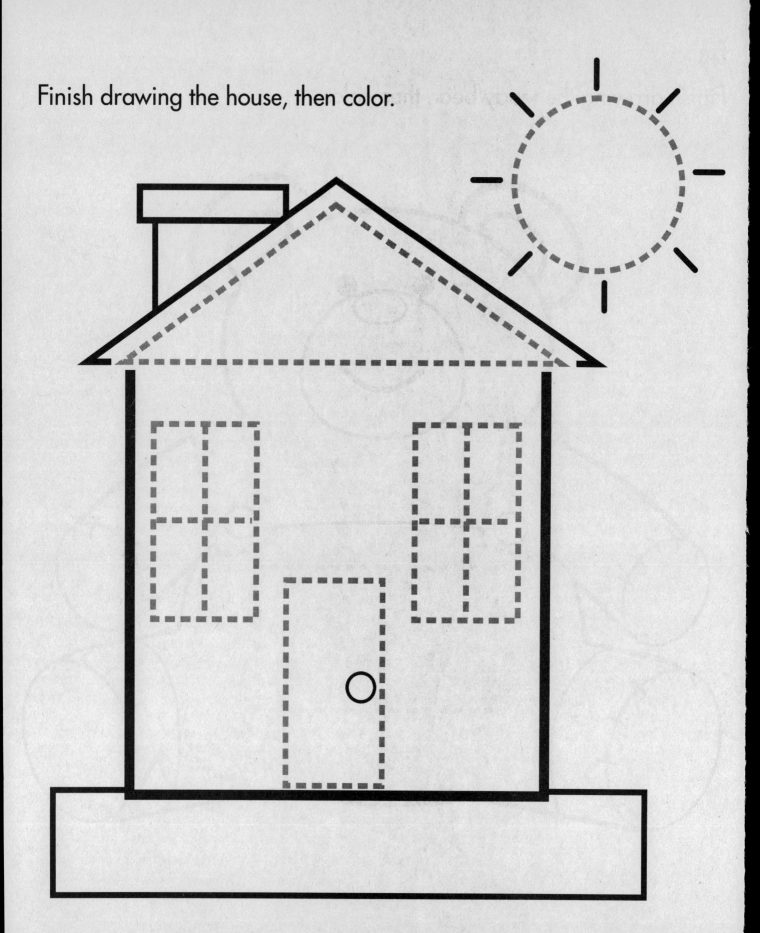

What shapes do you see?

Finish drawing the flowers, then color.

The flowers have oval petals.

Finish drawing the ball, then color.

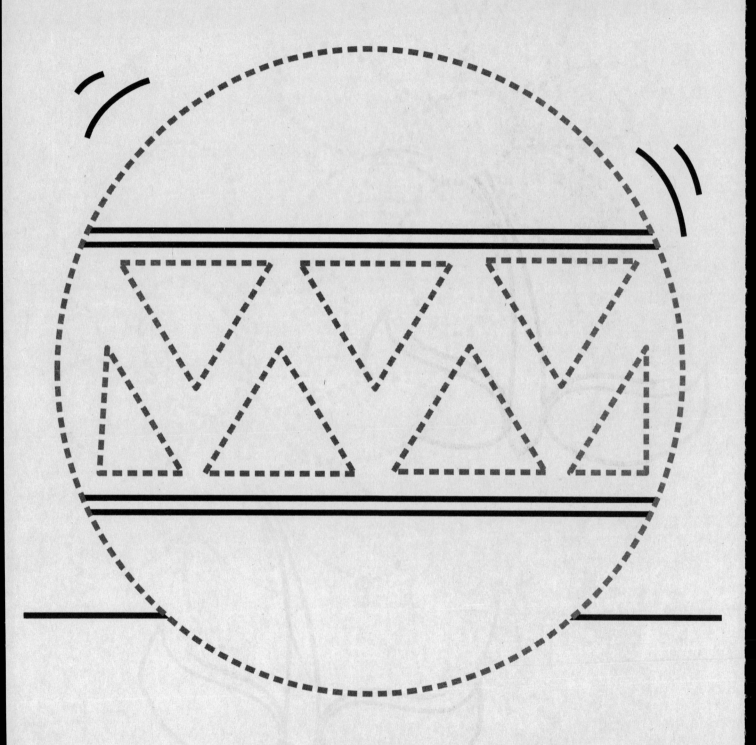

How many **circles**? How many **triangles**?

Finish drawing the juggling clown, then color.

The clown likes **circles** and **triangles**!

Finish drawing the gumball machine, then color.

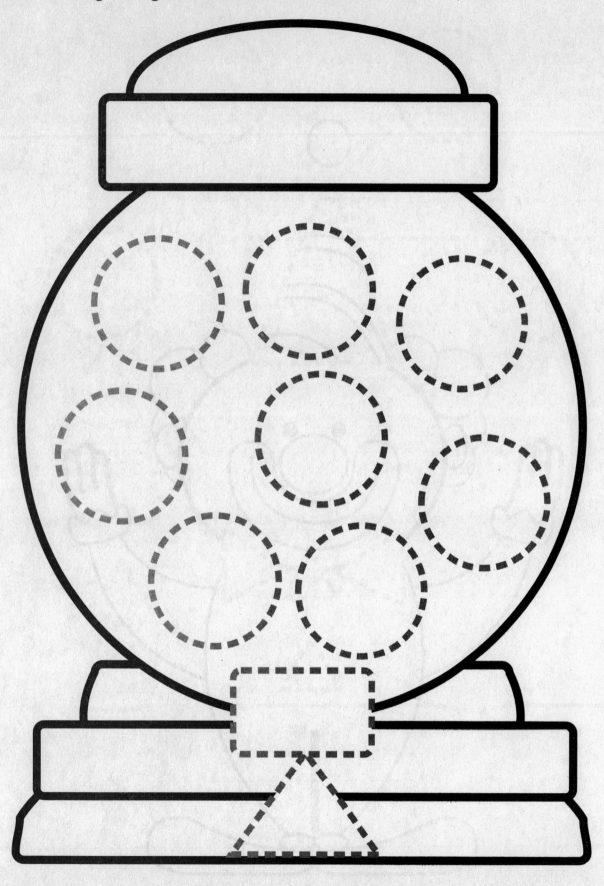

How many **circles**? **Triangles**? **Rectangles**?

Finish drawing the truck, then color.

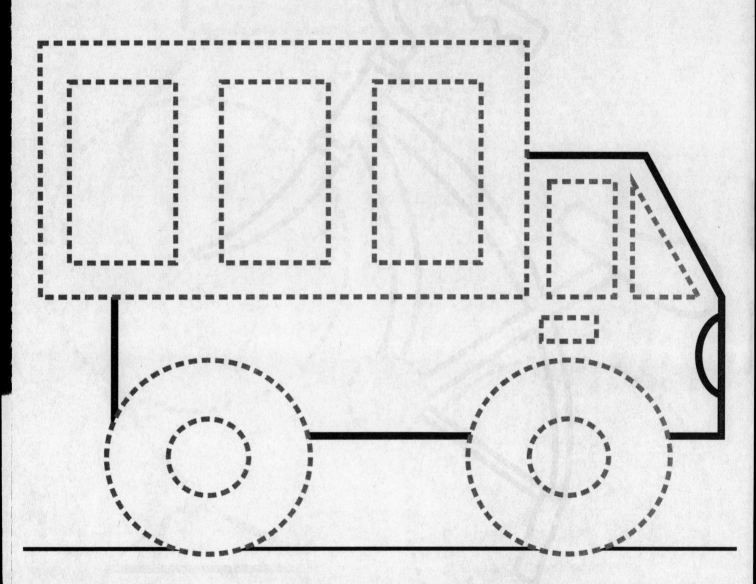

Can you see lots of shapes in the truck?

Finish drawing the bicycle, then color.

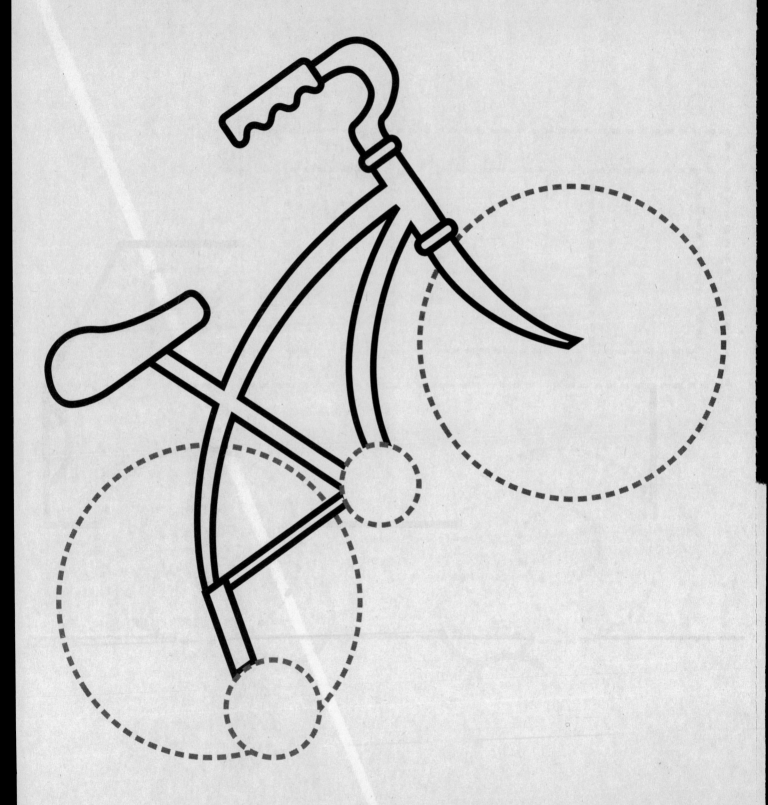

Can you see **circles** in the bike?

Finish drawing the robot, then color.

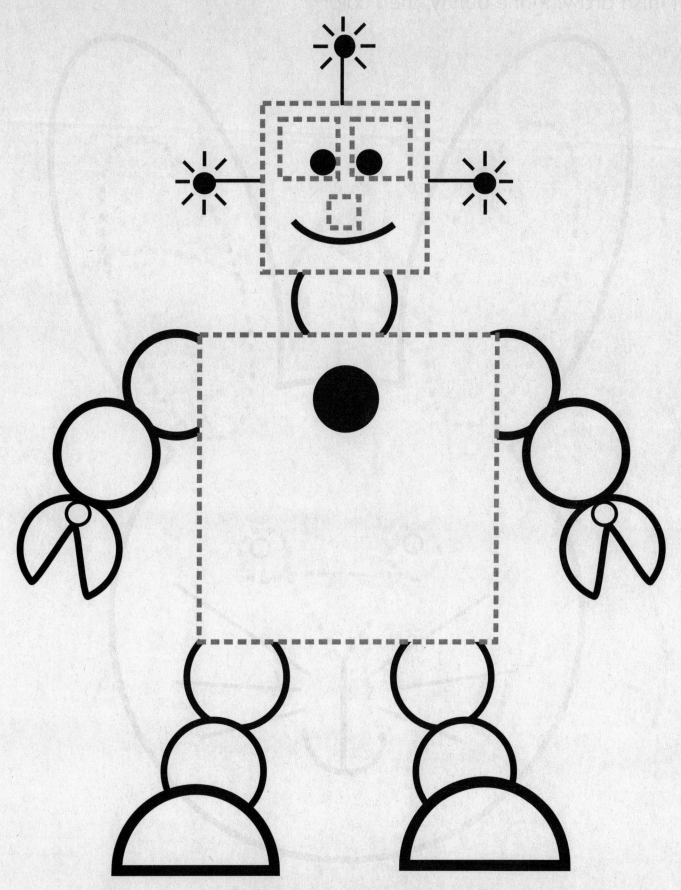

The robot is made up of **circles** and **squares**!

Finish drawing the bunny, then color.

What shapes do you see in the bunny?

Color Key

= blue

= green

= red

= orange

= yellow

= brown

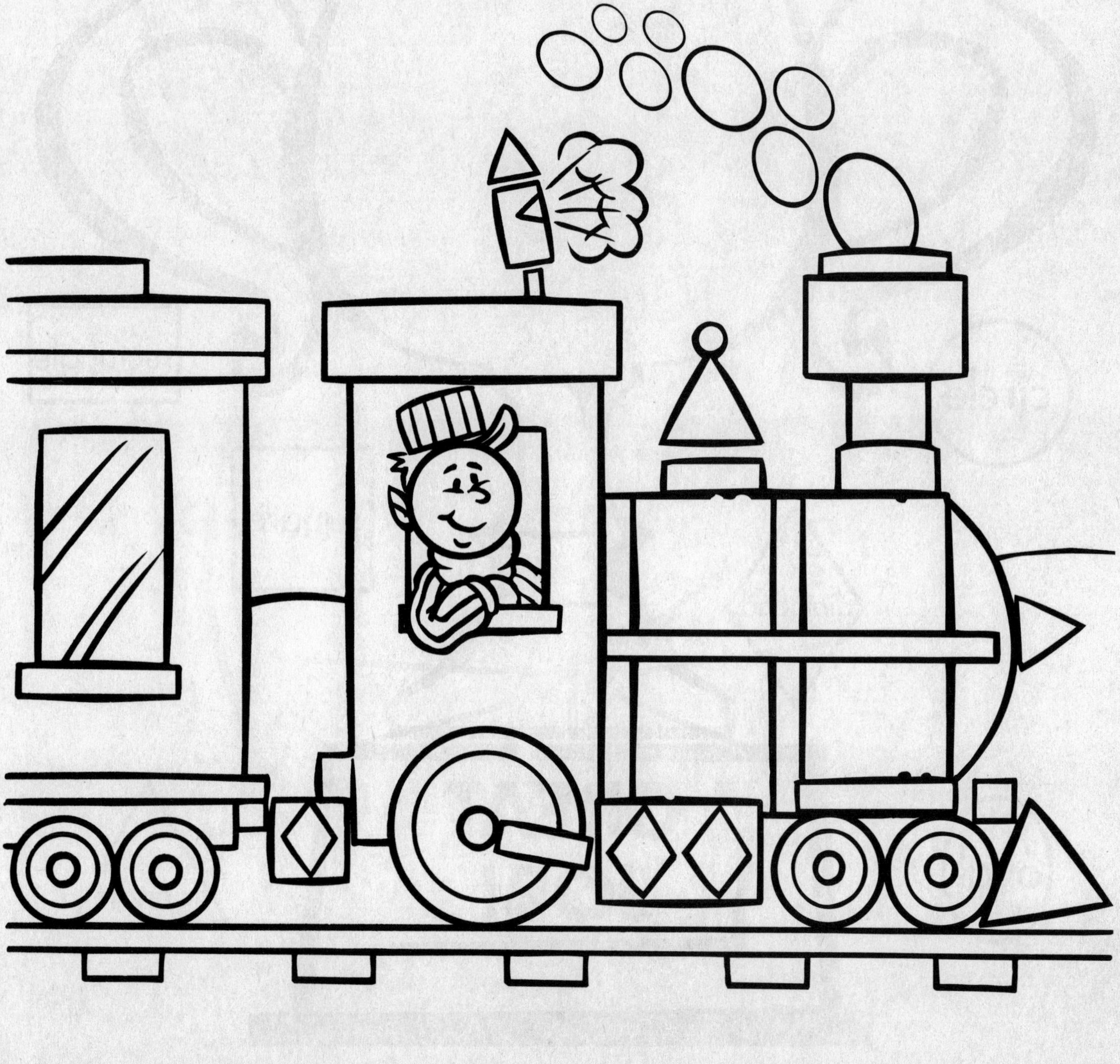

You are a shapes champ!
Write your name.
Color the trophy.

_____

Congratulations _____ !

circle

rectangle

diamond

square

oval

GREAT JOB!

triangle

Connect the dots from **a** to **z**.

Which climber can get to the top of the mountain?

STOP

START

START

START

Connect the dots from **a** to **z**.

Connect the dots from **I** to **20**, then color the picture.

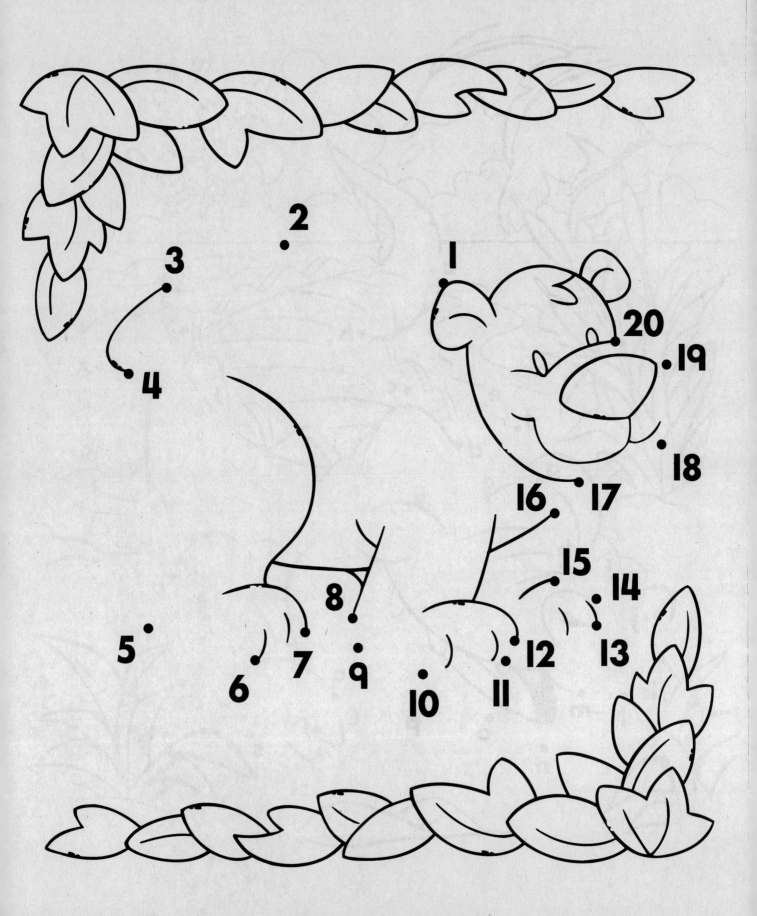

Letter Key

A = E = G = O =

U = R = T = Y =

___ ___ ___

___ ___ ___

___ ___ ___ ___ ___ !

You are a super learner!
Write your name.
Color the ribbon blue.

_____

Congratulations _____ !

Reading

Counting

SUPER
LEARNER!

Letters

Phonics

Shapes

Numbers

Colors